From Whiskey to Water

From Whiskey to Water

Sam Cowen

First published by MFBooks Joburg, an imprint of
Jacana Media (Pty) Ltd
First and second impression 2016

10 Orange Street
Sunnyside
Auckland Park 2092
South Africa
+2711 628 3200
www.jacana.co.za

© Sam Cowen, 2016

ISBN 978-1-920601-72-0

Cover design by publicide
Set in Sabon 11/15pt
Printed and bound by Shumani Mills Communications,
  Parow, Cape Town
Job no. 002795

Also available as an e-book:
d-PDF ISBN 978-1-920601-77-5
ePUB ISBN 978-1-920601-78-2
mobi file ISBN 978-1-920601-79-9

See a complete list of Jacana titles at www.jacana.co.za

"Someone I loved once gave me a box full of darkness. It took me years to understand that this, too, was a gift."
– MARY OLIVER, PULITZER PRIZE-WINNING POET, FROM THE POEM
'THE USES OF SORROW'

It took me still more years to learn that that person was myself. Thank you to all who helped me realise that and to find the light. I know who you are. I hope you know who you are too.

"I am still learning to love the parts of myself that no one claps for."

– RUDY FRANCISCO, POET AND ACTIVIST

"I walk around like everything is fine but deep down inside my shoe, my sock is falling off."

– UNKNOWN

Acknowledgments

This book has been a long time in the making – not in the writing of it, but in the living of it. Fourteen years is a very long time and gratitude has to be extended to all those who lived through it with me and loved me anyway.

To my family, near and far: sometimes I have dragged them, sometimes they have dragged me, through all my adventures, both anticipated and unexpected. Special mention to my lovely husband who did more diets than is humanly decent and my children whose perspective has helped reframe my own.

To my friends: those who were there before the storm and sailed through it and those who met me since and accepted it. There are no words to describe how much I love you.

To those individuals who allowed me to use their stories in this book: I have deliberately changed names and places and kept descriptions to a minimum but I hope I have done you all justice. Often it was your generosity that saved me.

To a fantastic publishing team: thank you, Melinda Ferguson, for inspiring me, for believing in this and pushing it for months. And thank you to Sean Fraser for an amazing edit. This book is better because of you. Thank you, too, to all the behind-the-scenes people who make books possible.

To all the swimmers, the people I swim with often and those on the periphery. You all inspire me over and over. You all know who you are.

Preface

My daughter is eight when my secret stops being a secret. I am driving her and a friend home for a sleepover when it occurs to me that my secret is no more.

"Bella," says Genevieve casually, "my mom used to drink *lots* of wine."

My fingers tighten on the steering wheel.

How does she know this? We've never told her that. We told her Mommy is allergic to alcohol. Mommy can't have a glass of wine or a beer like other people because she gets sick and has to lie down. We have edited out how Mommy also used to throw up and make promises to host huge lunches that she would then forget or sometimes drove home on the wrong side of the road or fell asleep in car parks and had all her friends panicking for hours as to where she might have been.

"Really?" The little friend is both cheerful and curious. "How much is lots?"

My daughter is full of information.

"*Lots*. Like *so* much. Like TONNES."

I don't correct her on her unit of measurement. I don't say anything at all. I just keep driving.

Genevieve continues.

"Luckily, she stopped drinking before she got pregnant with my bruvver or he would've been born stupid. And then I could have told him he was stupid and it would actually be true."

I step in gingerly.

"Now, darling, we don't call anyone stupid, because that's not very nice, is it?"

But the eight-year-old is having none of it.

"It might not be nice, but it would be true. He would be stupid and have to go to a school for stupid children."

Clearly she has a working knowledge of foetal alcohol syndrome.

I don't remember much more about the journey home. I do know that my alcoholism is now classroom conversation. And that perhaps that merits a further conversation at home.

So, at home, I tackle my 11-year-old. Christopher is playing DragonVale on his iPad. This is both time- and attention-consuming.

"Chris, how much have you told your sister about Mommy's drinking?"

Chris knows more than Genevieve. He knows I haven't had a drink in over 13 years and he knows a little about why. He knows I would lose both memory and time, long stretches I could not account for. He knows it was very bad for me and made me sick. He knows it upset Daddy. But, as far as I know up to this point, that's all he knows. I need to know if there is more.

Silence.

"Chris, I'm talking to you."

"I've got a new dragon. It's a Kairos."

"I don't care. How much have you told your sister about Mommy's drinking?"

Silence.

"CHRIS!"

He eyes me coldly.

"This dragon is *very* difficult to get."

And this conversation is *very* difficult to have.

"But have you told her I'm an alcoholic?"

"I don't think so. Maybe Daddy did. Can I just finish this level?"

He does not care how his sister knows. He does not care at all. As long as he has been alive I have never had a drink. Never smelled of wine. I have never woken up and not recognised him or had to explain why I am home late or why I am still in the clothes I was wearing yesterday. He has never seen me drunk. It is not relevant to his life. Certainly not as relevant as DragonVale.

"Does it bother you?"

"No, because I've got it now."

"What?"

"The dragon, I've got it now."

"No, I mean does it bother you that I'm an alcoholic?"

He turns to me in irritation.

"Are you still talking about that?"

"I'm trying to be a concerned mother."

"Well don't. It's weird."

And that's that.

Later, when I'm alone with Genevieve, I ask her how much she knows.

"Darling, who told you that Mommy used to drink so much wine?"

I tend to talk about myself in the third person when I am with her.

She shrugs.

"I don't know."

"You don't know or you don't remember?"

"I don't know and I don't remember."

Well, all right then.

"Should I make the kitchen pink or purple?"

She too is an iPad child. She turns the screen towards me.

"I like pink, but I still want to ask ..."

"I like purple."

So the kitchen is purple.

I plough on.

"I just want to know how that makes you feel."

Her green eyes turn to me, and she smiles widely.

"It feels good 'cos I like purple more than pink." She slides her finger across the screen like lightning. "But you *can* have pink chairs at the table."

"No, I mean how do you feel that Mommy used to drink a lot, but doesn't any more?"

She looks at me blankly.

"I feel good?"

It's a question because she doesn't know the answer. And I'm very grateful because it means that the idea is as foreign to her as another country.

"Well, that's good," I say.

"Yes. Now I am making a cave."

And back to the world of Minecraft goes my daughter.

But there's one more person.

"Martin, did you tell the kids I'm an alcoholic?"

He blinks at me over his glasses.

"I don't know. Probably."

"*Probably?*"

"Well, yes … They were going to find out sometime."

And of course they *were*.

My name is Samantha and I am an alcoholic. At the time of writing, I have been sober for 13 years, 11 months and 16 days. And, yes, I still count. And I'm writing about it now because I promised myself that I would once my children understood what that meant, that Mommy was an alcoholic. I think they may have understood long before I did, even if all the details are the stuff of ancient history for them.

So this is the story of how I stopped drinking.

No, it's not.

It's how I stopped drinking, started eating, became clinically obese, stopped eating (everything that wasn't nailed down) and swam my way to freedom.

No, it's not.

It's about addiction and learning and sadness and anxiety and love and drive. It's about channelling the unchangeable into the miraculous. It's about dragons and learning how to put them to sleep when you can't slay them. It's about being my own Daenerys.

PART 1

Drinking

CHAPTER 1

Thinking

"You don't drink like other people."

That was the first time I ever really thought about it. About my drinking and whether or not it was a problem. It was in 1995, after a 702 concert at the zoo. I had had the mother of all fights with my flatmate Zev – I still don't remember exactly why. We were sitting in my car at Zoo Lake, in a dark car park opposite the zoo, and let rip at each other. Was it because I'd forgotten where I'd parked the car and we'd had to walk forever? Maybe. It wouldn't have been the first time. Or was it something he had done or not done? Possibly. He wasn't always an angel either. But it didn't matter because the fight ground to a halt when he said that.

"You don't drink like other people."

I hadn't thought about my drinking before that. I did drink a lot and when I drank, I *drank*. But I was 21, didn't everyone at that age? I worked in a pressured newsroom; I worked intense shifts. It was a crazy time in the country's history – everybody drank. There was an honour bar at work every Friday and a lot of us would gather there, propping up the counter, drinking beer and wine and hard tack at ridiculously low prices. And it wasn't unusual for us to take the party to one of the bars or clubs across the road or to the pub on the ground floor of the building next to us, an Australian-owned gastro-pub-type place called The

Outback. That's where we would go and have dinner and then more drinks and it was great. It really, really was. I was very shy before I joined 702. At university I flew under the radar as much as I could. I never left an impression; maybe more of a watermark. Everything made me nervous and anxious. But after a few drinks, the world got warmer and conversation got easier and it felt good.

"You don't drink like other people."

Didn't I? How did other people drink? It's not like I drank all day. I only drank when I was with other people. And, anyway, it was a fun day! It was *meant* to be a fun day. The wine was flowing freely – everyone was drinking. Even people with kids, although not as much, obviously. Those were the days before Uber and Good Fellas, but it was also a time where roadblocks were few and far between, so we didn't really worry about them. And, besides, it wasn't as if I was the biggest or the worst drinker that day. Someone else at the concert lost her car for real. She phoned me the next day to try to work out where she might have left it and, together with a few other people, we managed to piece together where it might have been. She found her car 24 hours later, nowhere near where she thought she had left it. And we all laughed! It was funny! And no one got hurt. It's not as though there had been an accident or anything.

"You don't drink like other people."

So why did he say that? How was I different to other people? I didn't understand. But it was the first time I wondered whether I was indeed different. Whether wine made other people feel as happy and confident and relaxed and … calm … as it made me. Whether, when other people drank a glass of wine, their fear centre shut down and their happy place rolled up the shutters and opened for business.

I asked Zev what he meant. I probably shouted. He shrugged with irritation.

"I don't fucking get you, Sam. You're just different. I don't know this person. You just aren't … you."

But it was me. The process of flicking the switch from social drinker to heavy drinker to full-blown alcoholic had already started by then. I didn't realise it that night. But someone else had.

CHAPTER 2

Why?

You know that feeling you get when there's a letter from SARS in the post? And even though you know you've paid your tax and you're up to date on submissions and IRP5s and estimates and provisional this and value-added that, your heart sinks and your stomach twists an involuntary kitka? That, although you know absolutely nothing could be wrong, you still anticipate the worst? Well, imagine feeling like that all the time. All. The. Time. That's how I feel.

That's an exaggeration of course. No one feels sick all the time. Or frightened. No one's hands shake all the time. But that's how it feels. And at night, when I wake up and my heart is thumping so loudly I can hear it and my head hurts to touch it and my ears roar, I comfort myself with that fact. That it's not actually all the time. Not every minute. Or even every hour. Just most of them.

It comes when you least expect it, anxiety. It's not like fear. Fear you can see on the horizon. It's like a pirate ship – there's always a chance you can avoid it or fight it. Fear is rational. It comes from somewhere. Or something. It's based in reality. Panic is not. Panic is what you feel when your entire mental processing system is overridden. It's when you know that if you were comforting someone else, you'd be able to rationalise and maybe even joke about it. You could tell them to calm down. Tell them, it's never as bad as you think. You could say, this too shall pass. But not when it's happening to you. Not me.

I panic a lot. I always have. When I was little I panicked that my mother would die, even though she was perfectly healthy. I panicked that Ronald Reagan wouldn't win the US presidential election in 1984 and there would never be an end to the Cold War. I panicked that I wouldn't be good enough to go to heaven if I died suddenly. Now that I'm an adult I worry about different things. Some days it starts with something real, like an inexplicably high electricity bill, and then settles into its own loop. Like an old car radio where the knob to change channels has snapped off and you're permanently stuck on one station and it's always on because, even if you hate it, you can't turn it off until you turn off the ignition.

And at first I have the energy to deal with the angst. I'm an intelligent woman. I tell myself all the things I would tell someone else. It's not your issue, Sam. You can't own this. You can't take it on – you can only control what's yours.

I can sort out crises for others with some well-chosen words, a non-judgemental approach and a series of hugs. But I can't do that for myself. Because that panic has its own life force. Like some kind of drunken zombie, it lurches from real problem to imagined wrong to supposed weakness, infecting everything. All of it. So eventually, in the middle of the night or just before dawn, I'm as terrified of being late for work as I am that I won't get my leave forms in on time or that I don't know where my passport is and I really need to look for it. Urgently. And then I get really frightened. Why? Because I get out of bed to go and look for it. That's what I do – go and look for it. Even though I know where it is. And it's the act of getting up and searching that makes it worse – that if I could be worried enough to get up and look then maybe it is an issue. And now it's a whole new issue I will have to worry about. Something else to manage. Or to control.

Control. Now that's the Big Bad Bear. Because it's a short-term panacea. If I can control the problem, it isn't a problem. So if I know where the passport is, if I can be sure I'm not letting anyone down or revealing this pit of sticky black need, then it will be okay. At some point, some time, it will be okay. And that's why I obsess over the little things, those silly poisoning little things I can manage. I can own. Because if I can get that right, surely the other stuff will follow? Won't it?

Sometimes I wonder if I can punch in a different code. Like the combination lock you get on hotel safes where you can reset the code for every guest. Press reset, enter your own code and voila! New security. Perhaps that's what I need – new security. If I could key in a different code, I wouldn't be like this. So rigid. So determined to stay within the lines. So obsessed with the safety I find in the order of little, meaningless, petty things. Because I do find safety there. There's a hysterical kind of order to it. If the house is clean, everybody is fed and there's water in the taps and power in the light bulbs, I've done it. The train's on its rails. But it's an exhausting process.

I don't tell people this. I don't think many of them would believe me. I do not look anxious and I have no reason to be. I am lucky. And I make jokes about being neurotic, but very few people have an idea of the depth of the problem. And I've always been afraid they will find out; that they will realise I'm a liar, a fake, a fraud, an imposter. I am not brave or witty or clever; I am just a good actress. And one day everyone will know. But if I keep the little things together, oil the smaller cogs to keep the big wheels moving, I'll scrape by. So I keep searching for boxes to tick to prove to myself I have worth.

I don't do it to be difficult. I don't take pleasure in finding mistakes. I am not triumphant when I find a plate with a half-eaten sandwich on Christopher's bottom bunk. I don't enjoy the confrontations I have with Genevieve over why she shouldn't leave her shoes in my bathroom. Or why I feel such immense irrational sadness when I find wet towels on the floor instead of hung up on the towel rail. Or how, when I hang them up myself, I sometimes press my face into their dampness and cry and tears soak into them until I clench my fists in the cloth, willing them to stop. And eventually they do.

On energetic days, when I walk through the house and see the wet rings left on the coffee table, the crumbs on the kitchen counter, I want to scream; on other days, I want to weep. Is this my default setting, the Crumb Police? On duty 24 hours a day, seven days a week, ready and waiting to swoop on the unclean, the untidy and the disobedient. Which, of course, I don't, because it is not their fault. I am not their fault. I have two friends who are sober now. One was sad before he became a full-blown alcoholic; now he is sober, but still sad. The other was a hyper-excitable crazy woman. She took heroin to calm down. Now she's sober, but she is still a hyper-excitable crazy woman. This was me. I was an anxious, panicky person who drank to calm down. Now I am sober, I am not calm any more.

Some days I am a silent buzztrack of moan. "Pick up your shoes! Where are your books? Get off that computer! Get in the bath! Get out the bath!" I wonder where my factory settings went wrong. Why dry towels became my standard of calm. And yet they are, as are clean dishes, neat beds. They are important. So important, in fact, that I am more frightened by dropped towels than I am by the fact that I cannot sleep through the night and that I count to 10 more times in a day than a Grade 2.

That is how I feel when I am anxious. I know there are medications for it. And I take them religiously. Sometimes there are more and sometimes there are less. They don't take it all away, but they insulate me. They wrap it all up in cotton wool. But that just distances it all from me – it doesn't end or go away entirely. It will be there all the time, like a corpse in an open grave. Medication might cover it up and plant grass and put up a nice tombstone, but the body will still be there. Waiting to be dug up. So I carry on, a loop that goes around and around. I thought I could dissolve it in a glass of wine, but when the glass was empty it was still sitting at the bottom.

I drank for all the reasons I don't drink now. When I started drinking it was for fun. To fit in. I only drank socially and really not very much. But I loved the way it made me feel. I loved being part of something. The whole point of selling beer in a sixpack is so there is something for the other five of you. A wine bottle services five or six glasses. There's a sense of camaraderie in drinking with other people. That's what watered the seed, I think: that a drink was a passport to a new country, with new people. A friend who has stopped smoking four or five times insists that each time she goes back to it, it happens at work.

"You see everyone standing outside on the balcony," she says. "And you just want to be out there with them."

I ask the question, even though I know the answer.

"Why not go out there anyway? You don't need a cigarette to have a conversation."

She looks at me resignedly.

"Because it's not the same. It feels like them and me. Before, it was *us*."

She says the best times were in winter because only the die-hard smokers ventured outside in the cold. They would huddle together like birds on a telephone wire, blowing on their hands and taking long drags, trying to make each one count so they could get back inside quickly – only to come out again an hour later. It was a ritual.

There's an episode of *Friends* in which Rachel pretends she is a smoker just to get close to her new boss. Clasping a cigarette in hand, inhaling uselessly, she tries to wheedle her way into the group, the conversation, the clique. I think that's how many of us start drinking. It's easier to make friends with people when you have something in common, especially if the thing you have in common makes you relax and feel confident and pretty and alive.

When I was 14 I tried smoking. A lot of my friends were doing it, but I was conflicted. It was expensive and bad for me, and it would upset my mother. She had a love-hate relationship with cigarettes. She enjoyed every single one she smoked, but spent most of her life 'trying to cut back'. But ... my friends. Eventually, I decided I would try it out in front of the bathroom mirror to see what I looked like. I waited for everyone to go out and then lit up one of my mother's Benson & Hedges Special Mild. I took a puff and then stood and watched myself trying to exhale. I didn't look like some mysterious fifties' film noir Hollywood starlet. I looked dreadful. I had, and still have, very short fingers, and I looked ridiculous, like a child who had stolen a cigarette – which of course I was. My eyes watered. I stubbed it out. I didn't end up smoking. Later I started drinking. By then I didn't care what I looked like.

Drinking was different. It was warmth in a glass. It allowed me to be my best self. Well, let's qualify that … It allowed me to *feel* like my best self and that varied depending on whom I was with. On my way out to a date once, I confided to my flatmate that I worried whether the man would like me or not.

"He'll love you, Sam," Zev said confidently.

"He doesn't know me," I said with trepidation.

"Just be yourself!" he called after me as I shut the door behind me.

Just be yourself, he had said. It sounded so simple. Just be yourself. Of course I would, but which self? Would I be the hard-drinking, hard-swearing, funny, caustic Sam, the girl who used to boast that her three favourite men were Jack Daniels, Jim Beam and Graham Beck and wear her shirts just a little too tight? Would I be soft, sweet Sam, understanding and caring and empathetic? Or cynical, worldly Sam, who produced a shit-hot current-affairs programme, the young, bright rising star?

And whichever one I chose to be, would she be the right one? If I misjudged, I could blow the whole evening. That would be bad. But even worse would be if I picked the right Sam for the date and then had to sustain it. I tried to be all things to all people, and on enough wine I thought I really was. I had loads of luggage on the baggage carousel, bags and bags, they were all mine and they were always moving and I had to keep an eye out for every single one.

One very sweet man I dated said he wished more nineties' women liked to cook from scratch. He said he knew a lot of people saw it as outdated, but he loved it. I don't even know how much I liked him, but I knew how much I liked a challenge.

"Well, I know it's not very nineties to admit it," I said, "but I love to cook! And I cook everything from scratch."

It was not a rare thing for words to come out of my mouth before the filter on my brain had time to edit them.

"Come round for dinner this weekend," I said confidently. "I'll cook something."

And he said that sounded great.

And it did sound great. There was only one problem. I didn't like to cook at all. And I especially didn't like to cook anything from scratch except pasta, which I would mix with sauce I had decanted from a bottle or a carton. That counted as 'from scratch' for me.

Never mind. There would be wine.

I inspected the frozen ready meals in the supermarket fridge. I knew it couldn't be a good old Woolies meal because he would know. It would have to be something he would never suspect.

So I bought a no-name-brand chicken chop suey. I made rice and put it in a steamer and then I boiled the chop suey, emptied it into a casserole dish with some cream and black pepper, and was all systems go by the time he arrived.

He loved it.

"What is this?" he asked appreciatively. "It's delicious!"

"It's chicken surprise!" I teased, half truthfully, because it was a surprise even to me.

"I've never tried celery in a casserole," he said.

I just smiled because, until he mentioned it, I hadn't noticed there was any celery in it at all.

He came over twice more. The next time I 'made' authentic Italian spaghetti bolognaise, slow cooked for six hours over a low heat. And it really was; I had bought it from the Italian restaurant up the road, where you could phone through your order and then take your own bowls and plates and they would fill them. The other time I made clam chowder with a twist. Tinned clams, tinned butternut soup, extra cream and a pinch of cayenne pepper. You can get away with almost any culinary aberration if you add the words 'with the twist' to the title. So I did.

We stopped seeing each other – possibly because I got bored with being Domestic Sam, or because he saw through it. I really don't know.

When you are sober you have no choice but to be yourself. You can shut the windows and draw the curtains but you cannot change the house. You have to work with what you really are because it is all you really have. You cannot hide behind the curtain. Drinking lets you live in lots of houses, and at one point I was working a veritable Wisteria Lane. It's exhausting though. And depressing.

"No one understands me," I would weep into my cat's hair.

He would say nothing of course. He was a cat.

But people have to know you to understand you, and if you don't know yourself, how can you expect anything different from anyone else? But I was years and years away from making the connection between the two. Years and bottles and blackouts away.

I knew drinking made me feel better. I thought it made me better company and I think, even now, that I was probably right. The company I kept was mainly hard-drinking journalists and the one-upmanship at the bar was legendary. Two colleagues I drank with had hollow legs. One was famous for having lost a work car on a drunken night out, when he and another newshound had ended up in a leather bar.

"It wasn't the branded car, was it?" thundered my boss when he found out.

It wasn't, of course. If it had been, I think Tim would have been in much deeper water than simply on the end of a warning letter.

The other was a woman with a cast-iron liver, the one who introduced me to Long Island Iced Tea – an evil mix of vodka, rum, gin and tequila. We were at a rooftop bar in Yeoville when I had my first one. I think I had finished my fourth by the time I found myself at the foot of a flight of stairs in another part of town.

Tim was all for leaving me there.

"She'll be fine!" he slurred, hanging on to the bannisters for support.

Rebecca refused to leave me.

"We can't leave her here. She's just fallen down a flight of stairs!"

"So? She's already at the bottom! It's not like she can fall any further."

Rebecca dragged me up the stairs.

"We. Are. Not. Leaving. Her. Here." Each word was a step.

That made for a great story. Sam was so funny! And such a trooper! And so bruised she could barely stand.

So, yes, drinking made me feel part of the pack and insulated me at the same time. I felt safer with a drink in me. Safe enough to be unsafe. I could stand back and watch what was going on, even as I made myself the star attraction. It was like watching a video of myself on perfect replay. As I've said before, it made no sense. And yet it made perfect sense.

CHAPTER 3

Memories/ Blackouts

Sometimes I remembered things. Sometimes I didn't. I had blackouts. There were many, and right up until the end, I was never afraid, although I should have been. I just thought they were funny. According to an Alcoholism Clinic and Experimental Research study, blackouts happen when a person's blood alcohol level concentration is higher than what is considered 'legal intoxication'. And alcoholic.org defines 'alcohol blackout or short-term loss of memory caused by alcohol' as 'when the transfer of chemicals is interrupted before memories of the events leading to and during the blackout even have a chance to form'.

The problem then is that a blackout doesn't mean only short-term memory loss and an unplanned lie-down. The person having the blackout can still walk and talk and sometimes even be lucid. I was pretty much always drinking above legal intoxication levels. And I have lost what must probably be days of my life. There are nights and days I do not remember and I'm not sure what was worse, the things I did recall or the things I didn't. Tom Waits summed it up in his song 'Time', when he said that the things you can't remember tell you what you can't forget and that's probably the most elegant way to describe the way it was.

There's a process you follow when you've tied one loose the night before. Firstly, I would wake up and check my phone. That was long before the advent of social media. Luckily. I had to rely on SMSes and call logs to see what I'd got up to. I'd go through the latter with a feeling of sick apprehension. Who had I called in the dead of the night? Or the early hours of the evening or the late afternoon? Sometimes I'd see an ex-boyfriend's number and wonder whether I'd got through or not, and whether I'd said anything inappropriate … or not. Or if I'd said anything at all. Sometimes I would call my brother, Nick, in London and have what I considered to be a perfectly lucid conversation with him. And sometimes, apparently, it actually was. And it would go on for hours. Those were some special phone bills, they really were. But, you know, everyone did it, didn't they? And actually lots of people did. Those early nineties were times of very hard drinking for a lot of people. Well, at least, the people I drank with. The more you drink, the lower you go.

One morning, after a particularly energetic foray into the wonderful world of Shiraz with my friend Sue, I woke up to find a McDonald's receipt on the bedside table. It was for a sizeable amount too. Over R200. My stomach felt raw, like someone had sandpapered it from the inside. That wasn't the usual feeling I had after consuming a truckload of fat and sugar. I crawled through to the kitchen and rummaged for the packaging to see what I'd eaten, but there were no cartons anywhere. I looked at the receipt and I couldn't understand it. According to the bill, we had ordered one of practically everything. There were burgers of every type, from Big Macs to Quarter Pounders. There were drinks and chips and nuggets with sweet-and-sour and barbeque sauce. There was even one of each sundae: caramel, chocolate and strawberry. So where was everything?

I got dressed. Well, more dressed. As usual, I'd passed out in half my clothes. I seemed to do that often; perhaps I lost interest halfway through or perhaps I felt I'd disrobed enough. Either way, I would often wake up in a bra and jeans or T-shirt and socks. Charming and classy. Said no one ever. I went to check the outside bin. Perhaps I'd chucked all the empty packaging in there. But, no, that was empty too. I called Sue.

"Hey hey!"

"Yeah, fuck you a lot. I'm dying. How much did we drink last night?"

I glanced over at the table. Four empty wine bottles and two glasses, one lying on its side in a puddle of wine, as though it had just given up. I knew how it felt.

"Four bottles."

"Holy crap."

I had to know.

"Listen, what happened to the stuff we bought last night at McDonald's? Did we go to your place to eat it?"

Silence.

"You don't remember?"

"Going to your place? Nope."

"We didn't go to my place. We got back to yours and had a fight and I went home."

I didn't remember that. I dimly remembered driving home. Emphasis on *dimly*.

"What did I do?"

I asked because she was cross. So whatever had happened was probably my fault. Or I had at least started it.

"You gave all the food to a beggar."

I looked at the receipt again. That was a lot of food.

"All of it?"

"Yes, Sam, all of it. From the milkshakes to the burgers to the chips to the ice cream."

Dear God.

"And he didn't even want it all. You just forced it on him."

"How did I force food onto a beggar?"

"You got out of the car and put it all on the pavement next to him. All of it. *All of it.*"

I didn't remember that either, but I wished I had. It must have looked hilarious, this poor man surrounded by more food than he'd probably seen in a week, not knowing whether to laugh, cry or run away.

"Sorry."

"Yes, we went out hungry and came home hungrier."

I laughed. I couldn't help it. Even while small men with hammers worked very hard on mining inside my head, I laughed.

"How cross are you really?"

She laughed reluctantly.

"Yeah, okay, it was funny. But I was starving! And the next time we drink like that we're ordering in!"

The next time we drink like that. We knew there would be a next time. It was inconceivable that there wouldn't. And it was funny. So many things are funny afterwards. I would laugh along with others when they said, "Do you remember when …?" and I'd try not to think too hard about the fact that they were laughing because they remembered some hilarious occurrence and I was laughing because it was the first time I had ever heard the story. That memory was gone. My brain was like Swiss cheese when it came to drinking. I'd had the blackouts from early on in what I thought of as my drinking career. It was worrying occasionally, but I didn't let myself think about it too often. Instead I would comfort myself with what quickly became something of a mantra for me: "This sort of thing happens to everyone."

But it didn't. Not to everyone. Not to very many people. Just to me.

I became a bit of a Sherlock Holmes when it came to my own missing pieces. One morning I woke up clutching a toy duck – a big yellow fluffy one. How had I got this duck? I was a little worried, not because I was clutching an unfamiliar toy that had not been there the day before, or that it had obviously come into my possession during a bender, but more because I hoped I hadn't taken it from a child. That would be bad. I had visions of wrestling a soft toy from a toddler. I was 23, I could drink and vote. Please don't let me have relinquished my adulthood to bitchslap a child out of his or her snuggly. That might mean I Had A Drinking Problem. No one who just likes an occasional glass of wine or whiskey or vodka would snatch a toy from a child. I hoped against hope. With a sick feeling of dread, I phoned Sue, whose party it had been. Was it a party? Actually, maybe it was lunch. A lunch that evolved into a party. Or maybe it was only me who had seen the party side of the lunch.

"Uhm ... how did I end up with a duck?"

"That was the witblits."

The best definition for the term 'witblits' I've managed to find is that it's sorta kinda the equivalent of American 'moonshine', an illegally distilled liquor that can be up 50% proof or more, except moonshine is made from corn and witblits from grapes. But don't let soft fruit fool you. Not for nothing does it translate as 'white lightning'. That stuff is lethal.

But Sue's mention of witblits had jogged my memory. I remembered a little more about the day; there was a very annoying man at the lunch/party/mess. He was loud and overbearing and brought a bottle of the murky stuff he'd filched off someone at a hotel in Polokwane where a group of what sounded like equally irritating men had been playing a drinking game. This I remembered clearly. Just not how I ended up drinking it. Or going home with a toy duck.

"He dared you to match him shot for shot. And you did. Which we all thought was mad."

Yeah, that was mad. He was huge and I was not. And when it comes to holding your alcohol, the bigger you are, the better you are at it. What was I thinking? Obvious answer: I wasn't.

"And then you said you had to leave so you wouldn't have to drive home drunk. And you took my sister's duck."

So what part of that sentence should I have latched on to? The first bit where I drink loads of illegal spirit and then drive? Or the second where I experience relief that her sister is 27 years old and therefore couldn't possibly have spent the evening sobbing brokenheartedly over a stolen duck.

"Why did I take her duck?"

Sue laughed.

"Because you said you didn't want to drive home alone!"

I laughed too. Made perfect sense. Mystery solved.

I can't remember now whether, at that point, I knew this was weird. I don't think I did. The stories were good, even the one where I drank alone at home and woke up on the floor of the study, clutching the computer mouse. When I pulled myself up onto the chair I discovered I had tried to order a French maid's outfit from some American website. Luckily, I had forgotten my credit card number, or couldn't find my purse, or thought I had submitted it correctly but hadn't, which – considering that even 20 years ago it was nearly $60 – was a good thing ...

And, besides, I could tell a good story! I still can; I can take a tiny, insignificant event and turn it into a narrative masterpiece. Ever the comedienne. Ever hiding.

Some stories weren't so funny, though. During one in particular I wished for a blackout.

I did the odd bit of freelance work. One client in particular was incredibly tardy with paying my invoice. Every time I asked for my money there was another excuse, quickly followed by a dinner invitation. I didn't want to have dinner with him, but I seldom turned down a drink. So we had a few drinks. He was a fat, friendly, funny guy. But something was off. He looked like a teddy bear, but every now and again there would be a story that didn't sit right. He once told me how he'd met a prominent actor who he had a lot of dark secrets he couldn't possibly repeat. But I knew the actor and his past was about as dark as a fluorescent light bulb. Fatman didn't know I knew him. Fatman liked telling stories in which he was the hero. But after six beers, who cares? Each time we met, either he had forgotten my cheque – yes, in those days we were still paid via cheque – or he was going to do a direct deposit. He always had a reason for us to see each other again. But this time he had it in hand, or so he said.

In hindsight, what I did next was stupid. I didn't want to spend time alone with him any more. My mild ill ease with him had grown and I'd already decided I wasn't going to see him again, cheque or no cheque. So I invited him to a drinks party at my flat. There would be at least 10 people there; I wouldn't have to spend much one-on-one time with him and he'd pay me and go. That would be the end of it. Yes, he would know where I lived, but I wouldn't invite him around again, and I lived in a secure complex anyway.

When I asked him if he'd like to join the party he jumped at the invitation. But he didn't arrive. There were drinks, obviously; there was food, luckily; and there was great company. And secretly I was pleased that he hadn't turned up. I wrote the money off. It had been months of waiting and it wasn't worth it any more. I also had a growing suspicion he had been holding out on purpose, keen for a drinking partner with breasts.

We drank a lot that night, as usual. And one by one my friends peeled off home and I decided to have an emergency lie-down on the couch and a cup of black coffee. An emergency lie-down and a cup of black coffee often warded off that unpleasant session on the bathroom floor, hugging the toilet bowl. I don't know how long I'd been prostrate on the couch when I heard knocking on the front door. I guessed it was probably about an hour after everyone had left because my coffee was ice cold. I struggled to my feet and somehow managed to reach the door. And, without asking who was there, I opened it.

The complex in which I lived was populated with young professionals. All the units were the same, differing by a few square metres at most. One-bedroom/one-bathroom apartments, perfect for people who worked hard and played hard and really just wanted somewhere to sleep and occasionally hold a braai. We all knew each other and it wasn't uncommon for us to wander in and out of each other's places. Most of us never locked the doors when we were home. I loved it there; I never had any fear of who might pop in or of when. That night was the last time I ever felt that way. Fatman stood in the doorway. He was swaying slightly. It's amazing what you remember when you *do* recall a drunken evening. It's like a series of unplanned Instagram filters, some of it in sharp relief in which you capture every detail; some of it in soft focus, maybe clear in the middle and blurred around the edges. Lo-fi vs Brannen.

I stood and looked at him. This was all wrong. The party was over ages ago – what was he doing here? How had he got through the gate without calling me?

"You're late," I said stupidly.

"Better late than never," he muttered, pushing his way past me into my home.

"Everyone's left, so there's really no point in you coming in," I said, feeling distinctly uneasy.

"But I brought your money," he said, shoving an envelope into my hand. "And you invited me for drinks."

If you're a vampire folklore follower – which is a bit of a guilty pleasure of mine – you might have read the urban legend that says a vampire can only enter your home if you invite it in. Until then, you are safe. But once you've let it in, it can stay as long as it likes. Sometimes a vampire will trick you into letting it in. I thought this at the time. He tricked me. But I did invite him in.

And then he was pushing me up against the wall and trying to kiss me and I was frozen. I didn't cry out and I didn't scream. I kept thinking, this isn't happening, this isn't happening. And if it is, then what have I done to provoke it? And that little sober voice in my head kept saying, "You let him in, Sam. You let him in."

We ended up in the bedroom. I don't know how long we were in there. It could have been just minutes, but it felt like hours. Panic set in and I fought and fought but he was over six feet and built to match, and he pulled my clothes off, piece by piece. He was drunk too, but he was still strong and I was not. I didn't have a game plan for being attacked at home. I'd never thought about what I would do if something like this happened. I never thought it would happen. I never thought about it at all.

The oddest thoughts raced through my mind. Does my underwear match and, if so, what a waste, because I will never be able to wear it again. I will never wear any of these clothes again. Do I fight him? Do I just let him do it me so I don't get hurt? Well, even *more* hurt. If I fight harder, will he give up or will he get rough? And the thought that now makes the least sense: I wished I was more drunk, much more drunk; then I might not remember this and, if I don't remember it, how bad could it be? A dreadful, never-to-be-repeated one-night stand?

And all the time he was muttering, "We both want this, we both want this." But I didn't want this. I knew I didn't want this.

19

And yet … I'd invited him in.

I resigned myself to it. I went limp. There was no way I could win a physical battle. I was little and drunk and weak. And he was big and drunk and strong.

And just at that moment of surrender he passed out. Just like that. I was naked and he was stripped down to the ugliest pair of Y-fronts I had ever seen. Suddenly his body went slack, his head dropped onto my shoulder and within seconds he was snoring. I couldn't believe my luck. I lay there stunned. And then I tried to get out from under him. It was the first time I understood the term 'dead weight'. I couldn't shift him, and I started to panic. If I woke him, the whole thing would start again, I was sure of it. And, again, he'd be strong and I wouldn't.

I couldn't lift him off me, so I started trying to ease myself out from underneath. It wasn't easy; he was sweaty, and it was like trying to slip out of wet jeans. And every time I felt as though I was making progress he would half wake and pull me into him and the Great Escape would have to begin again. By the time I got out from under him I was sober – not breathalyser, blood-test sober, but sober enough to understand what had happened and sober enough to know my problems were far from over. He was still there, face down on my bed, and there was no physical way I could make him leave.

I grabbed my bathrobe, tiptoed out of the bedroom and locked him in. And then I sat down on the couch and cried and cried and cried. The front door was still open. I didn't get up to close it. What was the point? The bogeyman wasn't outside any more – he was prostrate on my bed.

So, why didn't I call the police? I'd been attacked in my home. I was almost raped. And the almost-rapist was asleep on my bed. He was still there. That's all I could think: he's on my bed. He's still here.

But I didn't call the police. I didn't call because I was drunk. Because I was drunk when he had arrived and would still be drunk by the time they got to my flat. Because my make-up was halfway down my face and I looked like a frightened panda. Because I had invited him for drinks. Because I had let him in. Because there was a cheque in an envelope on the kitchen counter. Because, if I wanted a couple of overworked cops to take me seriously, I had done everything wrong. Because I didn't think they would take me seriously at all. Because I knew I would battle to believe my own story.

So I didn't call the police. I didn't call anyone. I was embarrassed and ashamed. I sat up all night in my bathrobe, cuddling my cat, who must have known how upset I was because he let me hold him for ages. And he wasn't that type of cat.

The next morning Fatman knocked on the bedroom door and asked to be let out. I opened the door to a sheepish, sweaty, dishevelled man, dressed and ready to leave. Almost as ready as I was for him to go.

"I don't remember what happened last night," he said.

"We must have been very drunk," he said.

And then he left, through the front door that was still open. And we never spoke to each other again.

And I drank for five more years.

CHAPTER 4

Knowing

"But how do you know you're an alcoholic?"

That's a good question, and it's one I am asked as soon as people find out I'm an alcoholic and that I've been sober for 14 years. Surely, if I've been sober for 14 years I can't possibly be an alcoholic. Perhaps it was just when I was young? And sometimes I smile and shrug and say, "Well, I just know." Like I know the sun rises in the east and sets in the west. Like I know I'm a woman. Like I know I have blue eyes and blonde hair. Well, it might be blonde – it's been so long since I started bleaching it, I'm not really sure any more. But of everything else I am sure.

"But are you sure you're an alcoholic?" they ask. Am I sure? Yes, I'm sure. I'm sure with every fibre of my being. It's not a phase. It's not 'something I'm going through at the moment.' I'm an alcoholic. I cannot drink responsibly. I don't know how.

How do I know? I know because people who are not alcoholics do not ever ask themselves that question, not seriously. Not during the day after the night before, not when they wake up in the night gasping for water with their tongue plastered to the roof of their mouths, wishing they hadn't had so much to drink during the rugby or the braai or the dinner. Not even when they go to work the next day feeling tender. For the last two of my drinking years I asked myself that question a lot – first weekly, I think, and then daily, and then daily and nightly.

I know because people who are not alcoholics wake up the day after a boozy dinner and take two Panado and then tell their office mates about the night before and they don't worry about what those people think about them. Because it's funny. Because it isn't a regular thing. I never told anyone about the night before. I was paranoid that they would guess the truth. That the night before wasn't an isolated event like a birthday or a farewell or a hen's party. The night before was just like the night before that and the night before that. That wherever I was, whether at my home or someone else's home or at a bar or a club or a party, I would have been drunk and I would have had a hangover the next day. It wasn't funny. It was normal.

I know because people who are not alcoholics accept that they can't drink while they are pregnant because it's bad for the baby, and gloomily – or not so gloomily – resign themselves to a sober nine months, with maybe a glass or two of champagne at their baby shower. They don't decide, as I did, that they can never have children because they know they are physically and mentally incapable of staying sober for that length of time. Nine months without a drink? It may as well have been nine years. It may as well have been 90 years.

I know because people who are not alcoholics never have conversations like this over lunch. I think I'd been sober for 12 years when the following conversation unfolded.

"So, if you found out you had two weeks to live, what would you do?"

There were about five of us at the table, I think. The other four were drinking, but I didn't mind. I don't mind generally. My problem was never with what other people drank. My problem was what I drank and how much.

Someone in the group had recounted a story about someone who had been diagnosed with pancreatic cancer and been given two weeks to live. It made all of us examine our own mortality.

I rushed in. That 'angels fear to tread' thing? Yeah, I'm one of the fools.

"I'd go straight to the bottle store." It was a relief just thinking about it actually. With two weeks to live, I wouldn't have to try any more. There would be no more tough evenings, desperate for a glass of wine, no more long lunches watching everyone else get boringly blotto and having to pretend to be interested the third time they told the same old story. But, even deeper than that, no more having to be vigilant all the time. I could let down the guard against potential triggers. Two glorious weeks of oblivion before the end. I wouldn't have to feel bad; it wouldn't be like a real relapse – I'd be guilt free! I'd have fought the good fight; it would be a very peaceful surrender.

"I'd buy a case or 10 of Shiraz and a dozen bottles of Jack Daniels and then I'd lie on the couch and watch old series reruns until the end."

It sounded amazing. Then I became aware of the silence. Four frozen faces looked at me across the table. Someone cleared her throat and said, "But, Sam, what about your kids? And Martin?"

I hadn't thought about them. I hadn't thought about them at all. And when she said that, my first reaction wasn't one of guilt or shame – it was resentment. I'd been a good person for years, hadn't I? I'd been sober for them for a fucking long time. And now I was expected to give them the last two weeks of my life? Why couldn't those be for me? Why couldn't I have what I wanted? I wanted numbness. An end to anxiety. To be so gone, so inebriated, so many miles down the rabbit hole that it might be weeks before I realised I'd died.

But that feeling is not normal. Normal people don't think of how great it would be to be able to embalm yourself while you're still alive. Normal people think of how they would spend time with their nearest and dearest.

And that's how I know I'm an alcoholic. Because until the day I die, my body will still see its nearest and dearest in the bottom of a bottle of wine.

I know because I understand and relate to stories like this.

One man, also an alcoholic, tells the story of his own journey from blissful shame to uncomfortable sobriety. He was part of a group of men and women with whom I got together sometimes after AA meetings. For some people, the official meetings provide a place to unburden and offload and question, but for us they were a place to listen and to learn and to find mercy and understanding. Especially understanding.

"So for a while I thought I was a whiskey alcoholic," he said cheerfully. He was a big man, a 'boet'. Afrikaans and no nonsense. You'd never guess he had spent years waking up on the kitchen floor because to go to bed meant having to climb the stairs. We all nodded sagely when he told us that. No drunk likes stairs. Stairs come with a wealth of ways to fall down and then have to explain inexplicable bruises.

"I would drink scotch until I passed out. But when I had wine I was fine."

I laughed at that. This big Afrikaner – let's call him Boet – drinking wine. So unlikely. So like me.

"So then I thought I was a wine and whiskey alcoholic. Because I really got into wine, you know?"

Oh God, did I know.

"At first I thought, I could totally do this, this wine lark. Especially red wine. I even joined a Wine of the Month club."

And we all laughed at that. How we laughed! Wine of the Month? More like Wine of the Day.

"And it was cool. I drank it all. And I could talk about it. Like, I really knew my stuff in the end! I could tell you all about the different flavours and what the 'nose' was on a wine and all that shit."

And it was shit. It is shit. We all knew it. But he also knew it. That's how we all became so close. There was an old lady who used to carry a bottle of gin in her handbag wherever she went. On a good week, that would last her two days. She said she had joined Alcoholics Anonymous so she could learn to drink like a lady. Even before her first meeting was over she realised she would never drink like the lady she wanted to be, ever again. One of her ways of dealing with the day-to-day wobbles and fear and sobriety was to buy a tiny handbag. No room for gin in her bag; less room to fall down.

There was a young executive in finance. He didn't drink every day but when he did, he made it count. He had joined us when he realised that waking up in Durban when he'd blacked out in Joburg meant he had crossed the line from knowing how to party to not knowing how not to.

There was a northern-suburbs lady who looked the picture of efficiency. She was the kind of woman who could organise a dinner party for 10 gluten-intolerant vegetarians who were allergic to lactose and pull it off effortlessly. And she started each day with a shot of vodka. Just to get the wheels turning. She had managed to hang on to a luxury German car, but not her children or her home. She was staying with an aunt while her husband took care of the kids and they desperately tried to save a marriage built on years of half-truths.

And, of course, there was me.

"I used to take a case of wine to dinner parties in case there wasn't enough when I got there," Boet told us, nursing a cappuccino in his huge hands, "but I got away with it because I was the guy who knew his stuff from Wine of the Month club ... But you can't drink more than half a case yourself every time and not get noticed. One of my mate's wives said something. That was blind."

Yes, it would have been. Of course, he could have done what I did: finish a bottle and throw it away while helping to clear the table. No one would have known it was him, and he could have carried on the charade for much longer. Years longer maybe. But he didn't.

"Eventually I thought, nooit, I'll stick to beer. Cos, you know ... Beer."

Yes, we knew. Beer. Half the liquor content and lots of sugar and yeast to fill you up fast. The faster you fill up, the less you can consume. Well, that's the theory. But, for an alcoholic, those limits turn quickly into targets.

"And that was okay during rugby season, but you can't dop the same during cricket. Except at home. And who dops beer by themselves at home?'

Who indeed? Beer is a social drink. A few after work with the boys is okay. A few by yourself in front of the TV is just sad. And when you're sad, you start making the connection between what you're drinking and what you're feeling. And that's the most uncomfortable place in the world. That's when denial takes over like a headmaster who's just caught you cheating. Once it's caught you, you can never escape it.

"So then I thought I'll just drink coolers. Cos that's not really drinking. It's like Coke with a bit of a kick."

Boet drained his mug.

"But I knew when I came downstairs one morning feeling like shit and found 32 empty Hooch bottles on the kitchen table ... That's when I knew I had a problem."

And that is when he knew he was an alcoholic.

And the next day he went to AA.

I know I'm an alcoholic because the abnormal became normal. It became normal to drink a bottle of wine a night by myself. I was living alone at the time and I would drink alone. And that was normal, because who doesn't have a glass of wine when they get home at night? Maybe two? In my case, maybe six.

It became normal to throw the empty bottle in the bin outside so I didn't have to be reminded of it the next morning. I mean, who wants to dwell on that, right? Although at the time, of course, I didn't think of it as 'dwelling on that'. At the time, I thought of it as 'not wanting to clear up in the morning'. And yet ... the dishes would always be there waiting in the sink the next day.

After I got married it became normal to buy a case of wine and drink it all over the house. That way, my husband Martin wouldn't think I had had more than a glass or two of wine by the time he got home. He'd be right, in a way. I wouldn't ever have more than a glass or two from the bottle in the kitchen cupboard. I'd have had a glass or two of wine from at least three bottles: the one in the kitchen, the other in the living room, another in the bedroom. He didn't know about those though. It became normal not to mention it. Why would he need to know, anyway?

I know I am an alcoholic because my need for a drink sneaks

up like a mosquito in the dark. It's not attached to a situation or a person. It's a dull, annoying buzz that I cannot ignore or tune out. Sometimes I will be sitting in a nice restaurant, having a lovely time with good friends, under no stress whatsoever, with no underlying worries, where all is good with the world, and then someone will open a bottle at a nearby table and I'll catch a whiff. And the world will slow down and the conversation will dull and every sense will hone in on that lovely, intoxicating, delicious, dangerous smell and my whole body will hunger for it. And in that moment I will resent everyone and everything keeping me from it. Including myself. Especially myself. There's no rhyme or reason for it. I. Just. Want. It.

I know I am an alcoholic because the strangest things can trigger that hunger. Once, about six years ago, a friend who's a bit of a foodie bought me a bottle of alcohol-free wine. I hated alcohol-free wine. It tasted of fizzy apple or grape juice.

"Sam, this is new. It's made in the style of Cabernet and Merlot, so you get the taste without getting drunk."

I was sceptical. Highly sceptical. That rubbish fake champagne you get at supermarkets had made me suspicious of such lofty claims of paradise. But I agreed to try it.

I managed two mouthfuls of fake Merlot and had to pour the entire bottle down the drain. The taste was so close. Whoever had made it had done a dangerously good job. Memories came flooding back, memories of afternoons in the sunshine with friends feeling nothing but happy, and evenings on the couch with my cat feeling peaceful and numb, and dinner parties with people I didn't know feeling confident and funny – and I wanted it all back. I felt the loss so keenly in that moment. It was like I'd lost a part of myself. A best friend who protected me and improved me and comforted me. And I wanted her back so much. And I wanted the me that I was when I was with her. And I wanted a glass of real wine more than anything.

Almost more than anything. I wanted to be sober slightly more. But only slightly. And so, before anything could go wrong, before I accidently revved through an amber traffic light that turned red while I was in the intersection, I got rid of all that fake wine. And tried not to think about the real alternative. Not because I was relieved, but because I was afraid. I was eight years sober and I was as terrified of a relapse as I was when I was eight days sober.

There are many more ways I know I am an alcoholic, but I think the best way to describe my utter certainty is this: I still want a drink. Not all the time and not every day. Sometimes there will be a long time between those short scary bursts of desire. Sometimes there will be a few in a week. One year, I remember only one instance. I have nothing to drink away. I have a good job, a happy family and a lovely home. If I had continued to drink the way I used to, I wouldn't have any of that. I'd probably be jobless, homeless and loveless. And I know this. And I know how lucky I am to have the love and support that I have. And yet, knowing all that, I still want a drink. And that is how I know that, 14 years down the line, I am, at DNA base level, a proper alcoholic.

CHAPTER 5

Funny girl, funny drunk

It's amazing how, even 14 years later, I can laugh when I look back at some of my exploits. Embarrassing as they were – and are – I tell the stories as an illustration of how utterly wasted I was, even sober. I use them to explain to people why I can't drink moderately. I can't afford to try. And some of them will try ever so patiently to rationalise away some of the argument I have to make for myself that I am unable to control myself in the face of alcohol.

"I can't imagine you drunk."

"You're such a nerd."

That's my favourite. I am a nerd. Sober, I am the antithesis of Born to be Wild. More like Born to be Mild. And because my friends now are not my friends then, with very few exceptions. My friends now are mostly moderate drinkers. Like my husband, they can sit at a dinner table and nurse one or two glasses of wine over a four-hour period. Even now I marvel at that. I can't even nurse a Coke for a four-hour period. Sometimes they get up to leave *and there is still wine in their glass!* And I want to shout, "How? How do you do that? What's your secret?" Even now I want to know. I cannot fathom that.

They don't understand. And that's because they have never seen me drunk. So I try to explain. Sometimes. I tell them what you now know, about the sadness and the scaredness and the rock bottom. And they nod sympathetically, mainly at Martin, and ask whether it was really that bad. So then I tell them these stories. I tell them that this is what I was like when I was drinking. For years and years and years.

I was like a walking, talking, warped version of a motivational meme. "Never doubt yourself." I assure you that for years I didn't doubt myself at all. I was perfectly sure of my own abilities in the consumption department. Sometimes I got it wrong, but doesn't every expert in their field? It is from such mistakes that we learn and tailor our next moves accordingly.

Like the time I decided, in the middle of an *Inspector Morse* TV marathon, to drink an entire case of red. I blame Inspector Morse for that. He's the one who gave me the idea. He drank a lot of wine and whiskey in that series – really, a lot. I have no idea how he solved all those crimes in that series because most of the time he didn't seem sober enough to remember the names of the victims, never mind work out who had killed them. Bit of a fake, old Morse.

But, despite his flaw, I did appreciate his ability to imbibe. And I was a bottle or two down of a rather nice Pinotage when it occurred to me that I was probably a better drinker than he was. So far the booze hadn't really touched sides. I had a heroic tolerance for it by then. It wasn't at all uncommon for people to say, "Sam can really hold her liquor," and I took it as a compliment. And I thought it might be time to test that theory.

I went to the kitchen and carried the other bottles through into the lounge. It took a couple of trips, but that didn't put me off – it was like a warm-up for the main event. And eventually another 10 bottles of wine were lined up on the coffee table.

Ten green bottles standing on the wall, 10 green bottles standing on the wall, and if one green bottle should accidentally fall ... I'd be fucking pissed off.

At about four bottles, I realised I was getting really drunk and would soon be unable to do a Very Important Thing, which was to get the corks out of the other eight bottles. I thank God on a regular basis for the fact that in those days, very few wine bottles came with screw caps. If they had, I would probably be dead. As it was, removing a cork could be a ponderous business if you had lost a portion of your motor skills and, after four bottles of wine, I wasn't able to operate very much at all, forget heavy machinery like a corkscrew.

Let me open all these bottles now, I thought to myself. That'll give the wine a chance to breathe.

Breathe. Yeah, right.

But at least it sounded better to myself than, "Let me open all these bottles now before I cannot feel my thumbs."

That night I drank until I passed out. When I woke up I felt as though someone had ripped my head off and bounced it against a stone wall. Not that I've ever had my head ripped off and bounced against a stone wall, you understand, but I'm pretty sure that if it ever happens, that is exactly how it will feel.

I forced an eye open and looked over at the table. As usual, my wine glass had given up before I had. It lay in its customary position, on its side. Like a silent reproach. How could you leave me empty while you continued without me?

My bladder was so full I barely got to the bathroom in time. In fact, I used to time how long it took to urinate after a long night. My record is 49 seconds. I should mention that no one I tell thinks that part of the story is funny.

Back in the living room, I looked at the bottles on the table. Nine of them were empty. Nine. Empty. That's *seven hundred and fifty millilitres* times *nine*. That's over six and a half litres of wine. For some strange reason, there were also two bottles that were half empty and one that had lipstick around the rim so I'd obviously taken a swig or two out of that one, possibly so it didn't feel left out.

Rounding it up, I seemed to have consumed about seven and a half litres. I was slightly disappointed. I'd promised myself 12 bottles and I'd failed two thirds of the way through. Oh well, I'd fought the good fight. I'd gone down like a pro.

I corked the ones that were left and tossed the empties into the outside bin so my cleaner wouldn't see them. (That's another thing normal people don't do by the way ... They don't hide their evidence in the outside bin. That's because, for them, an empty wine bottle isn't 'evidence'. It's just an empty wine bottle.)

Argh. I hadn't made my target and now I would have to buy more wine. Disappointment all round.

Years later, I told an addict friend of mine about that evening. He refused to believe it.

"Rubbish," he said flatly. "You can't have. You'd be dead."

"I did! Would I tell that story if it wasn't true? It's not like it covers me in any glory."

Well, not these days anyway.

"Sam, you'd be dead," he repeated.

But I'm not.

Twelve green bottles. Nearly.

Then there was the time I went to visit my brother, Nick, in London and ended up curled up in a foetal position behind a dustbin. I should say upfront that I like London. I didn't drink only when I was stressed or anxious. I drank when I was happy and when I was excited and when I was celebrating and over dinner and special occasions, including days of the week, and when SABC started rerunning series of *Knight Rider* on Saturday nights.

And I did like going to London, even if it meant sleeping on my brother's couch in a commune he shared with a girl who worked at the council at Elephant and Castle and sang in clubs in Yugoslavia during the summer, and a man from Belfast whose claim to fame was to shit in a bag if the communal bathroom was in use by someone else, and leave it outside the door.

I liked drinking in London because the pubs in England are so pretty. They all have huge baskets of flowers hanging outside. Inside there are comfortable chairs that feel like they've been there forever, but sitting outside on a rickety bench drinking beer in the sunshine under a riot of shocking pink fuchsias was a uniquely lovely experience. And I did it a lot. I had a lot of friends in London besides my brother. Where better to meet than a pub? And beer was about the same price of coffee, wasn't it? And if you went to a chain you had to drink your coffee at tiny cocktail tables on barstools, and who wants to do that?

It's interesting to me that I was seldom drunk on those endless summer afternoons. Pleasantly mellow, yes, but not drunk. I'm still not sure why that was. Looking back, I wonder sometimes whether stopping then could have halted what now seems like the inevitable progression into the downward spiral, whether there was a formula I'd stumbled upon by accident for drinking moderately. Even if there was, it's gone now.

One night, when we were out with my former sister-in-law, I discovered raki. It's a Turkish drink made from grapes or figs that tastes of aniseed, and looks a lot like milk. In fact, it's known as Lion's Milk. Who could resist that?

You're not supposed to drink it with that in mind, of course. It's got probably the highest alcohol content of anything I've ever drunk. I don't know what it was that particular night, but it ranges from 45 to 90 per cent. I was down with that!

Maria was very scornful of my eagerness to try it.

"You'll pass out after two," she warned.

I watched Nick wince.

"I won't," I said hotly. "I'll fucking match you."

And apparently I tried.

The next day I woke up in my brother's lounge. He was sitting across the room from me drinking coffee.

"Well ..." he said.

"Well?"

"That was fun, wasn't it?"

Was it? I didn't think so. Nor did he. Nick's icy niceness when irritable could shatter glass.

"What happened?" I asked furtively, shifting a little on the couch. "Actually, I don't want to know."

He ignored that.

"Well, Sam, you tried to match Maria and two of her Turkish friends drink for drink."

He took a sip of coffee.

"I'm assuming I didn't."

"You assume correctly."

"Oh dear, I'm sorry."

"I'm not cross about that."

It was getting worse and worse.

"Dare I ask?"

He raised his eyebrows and took another gulp of coffee.

"Well, Sam, you had a little difficulty getting home. Actually, it would be more correct to say that I had a little difficulty getting you home."

"Were you worried I would throw up on the bus?"

"The buses had stopped running by the time I managed to convince you to leave."

I groaned.

"So we had to walk home."

And it was very far.

"And it is very far."

"I'm so, so sorry, Nick."

"I wasn't cross about that either."

Now I was worried. Like, really worried. Like, 'I'll never drink again but seriously I mean it this time' worried.

Nick gestured to a mug on the floor.

"I made you coffee and I suggest you drink it."

He continued.

"I was cross because halfway home you fell down."

Argh.

"You said you couldn't go any further because you were too tired."

I attempted a laugh.

"I probably was."

Nick didn't laugh.

"You were so tired you said were going to sleep in the street."

Okay.

"And I tried to tell you that you couldn't go to sleep in the street because, you know, it's the street."

He put his cup down.

"And you crawled behind a dustbin and said you would sleep there because no one would see you."

"I did not!" I couldn't have done that! Could I?

"You did do that. And you are too heavy to carry."

"So what did you do?"

"I told you I was going to call the police if you didn't get up and come home."

Oh.

"And still you wouldn't get up. So I got my phone out and pretended to call the police."

"And then what happened?"

"And then you got up and came home, crying all the way."

I tried a weak defence.

"It must have been a bit funny."

He eyed me sternly.

"It was horrible."

"I'm sorry."

There's really nothing else to say when you've done something like that, is there? It was like Jekyll and Hyde, if Jekyll was a bit of a drip and Hyde was more of a good-time guy and less of a rip-you-a-new-one kind of guy.

Nick's lips twitched.

"So I hope you're ashamed of yourself."

"I am, I really am."

Then he smirked.

"It was a bit funny."

Relief.

"Now today you can buy me lunch and then maybe I won't tell Mum and Dad."

I was 27 years old and still afraid of that.

"Nick, please don't! Please don't tell them!"

"Buy me lunch," he said, "and I will think about it."

So we went out for lunch. I was not allowed to drink raki.

But we did drink lots of beer under the fuchsias. And everything was all right again.

And he didn't tell my mum and dad.

Sometimes someone else's mum or dad told on me. Once my boss brought his kids to the office to spend the day with Daddy and they sat with me while he was in meetings. It was the morning after the night before and I felt really unwell. I certainly didn't feel well enough to deal with a barrage of questions from little people who are never tired and never bored and always loud. But I pretended.

The two boys stood next to my desk, bright eyed and expectant, aged about six and eight.

"What are those things?" asked the six-year-old cheerfully, pointing to a packet of used Brita water filters.

"It's something I haven't thrown away yet," I said blearily.

"Why haven't you thrown it away?"

"Because I haven't."

You can't get away with that with a child. I didn't get away with that with a child.

"But why haven't you?"

I gave him the bag.

"Why don't you throw it away?" I said with forced cheer. "That will be *very* helpful."

He tossed it into the bin with six-year-old enthusiasm. It sounded like a gong going off in my head. I groaned.

The eight-year-old looked sympathetic.

"Are you okay, Sam?"

I smiled weakly.

"I have a bit of a headache."

A bit of a headache that was the mother of all headaches ever in the history of headaches throughout all time.

"Are you sick?" he asked kindly.

"Uhm … maybe."

The six-year-old was having none of that.

"Daddy says you've got a headache 'cos you drank too much last night."

Thank you, Daddy. Fuck you very much.

37

Then there were wine tastings, the most pointless form of drinking there is. What's the point of swilling wine around your mouth and then spitting it out? It's like ordering food, Instagramming it and then sending it back! And I said so, at every wine tasting I went to. (Not the Instagram part. This was all before Instagram. But the premise remains the same.)

"Why all this foreplay and no follow through?" I whispered to the friend whose wine-tasting birthday party it was.

"I suggest we swallow it."

She was on board, as was every other woman there. We were ladies who lunched, me because I had a morning job that ended at 11 am and them because they ran their own businesses or worked from home or didn't work at all.

And all of us could drink. There was a wine called Versus and we mainly drank that because it came in one-litre bottles and was very reasonably priced! Such a saving! Such economy! And you didn't have to get up from the table so often to get another bottle.

Pippa once organised a wine tasting for her birthday. So clever. It meant that there was a lot to go around. I did wonder at some point if the sommelier realised how little we cared about the subtle blend of flavours or the 'nose'. I think she must have, because we were so bloody rude. We didn't care if there were undertones of chocolate or charcoal or hints of citrus. It was of no significance to any of us whether you could pick up the vanilla or the blackcurrant. Half of us had never tasted a blackcurrant.

I think she might have winced when we all added ice to our Merlot. But, it has to be said, it was very hot that day!

And the only thing that rivalled the pointlessness of swilling and spitting at a wine tasting was wine pairing. The only times I ever paired wine with food was when I was throwing up a combination of the two on the side of the road. Fish and Sauvignon Blanc left the least appalling aftertaste.

Then there was the time I rented office space by accident.

That was a good lunch! It was me, a former magazine editor and a PR person who was considering leaving her job. And wine.

Lots of wine. The magazine editor had quit her job and rented office space to pursue a freelance career as a writer, writing about things she cared about, which would no longer be leggings, skinny models or the 20 best positions in which to have sex. (I've always thought 20 was rather ambitious. Those articles make me feel horribly inadequate about the four or five I've managed to master.)

I wanted to be an author, the magazine editor also wanted to stop approving articles about very skinny girls wearing oversized clothes that would fit the rest of us quite snugly, and the PR person wanted to stop selling her soul, waxing lyrical about products and services she didn't believe in, like the washing powder that would make you want to quit your job to wash clothes all day and generally want to be a better person. So halfway through the meal we all decided that we would quit our jobs and work from our creative souls! Our talents would be able to thrive and grow in their purest form. We toasted our future success over starters, mains and desserts.

We would be writers of great books! Makers of great documentaries!

But not that day. That day we would fall asleep in our cars in the car park until the car guard chased us away to make room for the dinner crowd. Well, I would anyway.

The next morning, of course, I had forgotten all about it so when I woke up to a message on the answering machine telling me my share of the rent would be R700 a month, I had no idea what this woman was on about. Rent for what? Oh dear. I returned the call with trepidation.

"Hey hey! I'm so excited about this!" said the editor.

"Me too!" I pretended enthusiastically, pressing my head against the kitchen floor. Floor tiles. Always cool. Always comforting.

"Do you need the address? I can't remember if I gave it to you."

And I can't remember why you would be giving me an address anyway, but okay.

"No, you didn't."

I hoped that the address would give me a clue as to what I'd signed up for.

It didn't. It was for some anonymous office block in Westdene.

"And does it have everything there?" I asked cunningly.

Because 'everything' covered, well, everything …

"Ja, it does," she said excitedly. "There's a plug point for your laptop and a phone jack for if you want your own line."

I didn't own a laptop at the time. This might be awkward. Also, why would I need my own phone line? Was I starting a business? Cosmetics on the side?

"Well, let's hold off on that for now and just see how it goes," I said weakly.

And so I paid R700 for a desk I never used in an office I went to once.

Because telling her I had no memory of this ground-breaking creative decision really wasn't an option.

One night I got home from a night on the tiles, and while tripping up the garden path to my apartment building I was stopped short by the silhouette of a good-looking man staring at me from the window of the apartment block adjacent to mine. He was very good looking indeed. I stopped and looked. And looked and looked. Then I tripped a few more steps up the path and looked some more.

He was stripped to the waist, thumbs hooked into his jeans, hair like a lion, strong jaw, the epitome of hello baby. And he was staring at me.

I didn't know what to do. There we were, staring at each other! Him smouldering at me, me smouldering at him.

How had I never seen this man before? I had lived there for a year! Did he only go out at night? Or did he just smoulder out of the window at tipsy blondes? Who cared? He was smouldering at me!

I stumbled a few steps further, waving flirtatiously.

He didn't move. Just kept staring his come-hither stare.

Perhaps he couldn't see me properly? It was quite dark. I moved to the side of the path so I would be illuminated by one of the garden lights and waved again.

Nothing.

What was wrong with this man? I was waving! A young blonde in pretty good nick was waving at him! Why wasn't he waving back? Was he teasing me? Playing hard to get? I was determined to get a reaction, so I started to make my way towards the window.

And it was on that short walk that I realised that it was not a man I'd been fluttering at at all, but a poster of Jon Bon Jovi – a poster someone had stuck up facing out of the window instead of into the room. Oh well, saved by fan material. No one wants a one-night stand with a poster.

And what about the VIP tickets to Whitney Houston? That was a blast! I got mugged on the way to the stadium. In the car on the way there, I'd had a blazing row with my flatmate about him making us late by taking the wrong route. (He did and we were.) We were both still sulking as we moved with the crowd to our gate. The pre-show drinks we'd had at home beforehand hadn't helped. Sometimes drinking made me edgy, especially tequila. As we reached our ticket entrance, I felt an arm snake round my waist. I turned to him in irritation. I hated him so much in that instant.

"Don't even think about it!" I started to say, and then realised that the hand was tugging my wallet out of my pocket. In a flash, the pickpocket was gone – I could see him hurtling through the crowd. Spitting mad, my adrenalin levels shot up so high I was shaking. So I took off after him, Dutch courage powering me, even on the platform heels I'd picked for the occasion. On a normal day I would have stood no chance, but he had to shove his way through the crowd and he'd carved a path for me and I was gaining on him. Suddenly I had a brilliant idea – thank you, Olmeca – and took off my shoe and aimed it at the back of his knee. He went down like a ragdoll and rolled over, but before he could get up I was on top of him – literally on top of him, because I slipped and fell.

"Give me my purse this instant!" I shouted, trying to grab it from him.

He covered his face with his hands.

"Please don't hurt me," he begged.

I didn't. I took my purse, found my shoe and put it on. I felt like a reverse Cinderella. Except on tequila.

My flatmate was at my side.

"Are you okay?"

He gave me a hug. I loved him again.

We went into the stadium and up to the VIP box and straight to the bar. He ordered.

"Two gin and tonics. Doubles. Each."

Fuck Whitney Houston. I had Gordon's.

Oh, and getting lost! Find me a drinker who hasn't got lost. It happens to the best of us and to the worst of us. Little incidents like losing the car in a multi-storey car park, which still happens to me sober. That's why I always take a picture of my surrounds so I can find my car later – yes, really, I do. Now *that's* funny: drunk behaviour for sober people.

There were more serious occasions though. Like when I almost ended up in Kroonstad on my way home to Sandton from Melville. I know, I know, it's not possible. My boss at the time took out a road map of South Africa and demanded that I show him what roads I had taken. How could I show him? I didn't know! There were little roads and then a highway and then another highway and I think a toll plaza or two and the highway became a two-lane road and then a four-lane road – or the other way around, I don't know – and I ended up crying in a Shell Ultra. Or an Engen. It was a garage with a shop.

A guardian angel saved me that time. A great big man in a pink tow truck. He bought me a Coke and a Bar One from the garage shop and let me sit in his cab for a cry and I sniffed my way through the story.

"I'm going back to Joburg now," he said. "You can follow me."

Perhaps I should have been suspicious or at the very least cautious about his motives, but I wasn't. I was just ridiculously relieved and grateful. And yet again I was lucky. I got back in my car and followed him for what seemed like hours until I saw the lights of Johannesburg and the Hillbrow Tower and Ponte, and I knew I could make my own way home from there. And I did.

The problem with being a serial celebrator is that there are so many things to celebrate. Besides birthdays (yours and everyone else's), and new jobs (yours and everyone else's), and raises (usually just yours) and new babies, and the sex of the new baby and then the birth of the new baby and Christmas in December and Christmas in July, there is also the drinkers' paradise/Seventh Circle of Hell that is New Year's Eve. And that was a night I was in it to win it. I'd love to be able to tell you of my forays into the wonderful world of New Year's Eve, but unfortunately they've all run into each other, so here are some high/lowlights ...

The year I decided to drive home the wrong way down all the one-way streets from Rosebank to Sandton because I thought the police, if there were any, wouldn't be expecting that and I would foil any roadblock with such a cunning plan.

The year I had to be talked down off a table where I was doing the Macarena all by myself. I hadn't realised I was doing it all by myself. Apparently I was determined to stay up there until I had mastered all the moves. With the amount of melon vodka I had swirling around my system, it was a miracle I was even upright.

The year I had to be 'taken outside' a sports bar so a very kind friend could explain to me that meeting the band – as I had apparently been begging more and more loudly to do – was only possible when there actually was a band on the stage. What can I say? The sound system must have been very good that night.

The year I got so drunk I had to ask the toilet attendant to help me redress myself. Next time you're in a public bathroom, please tip the person there. You have no idea what these poor women have seen. That was the year 'the body' was in fashion. 'The body' was a leotard with press studs at the bottom, so you looked as though your T-shirt was painted on to you and not riding up your back as a common or garden T-shirt would do. There was only one problem with 'the body'. The more I drank, the less clear my vision and more impaired my fine motor skills and at some point in the evening I was so drunk that I couldn't match up the two sides of the fasteners. Because 'the body' was tight, you couldn't leave it undone or it would pop out of your jeans and you'd end up wandering round looking like a baby in a onesie needing a nappy change. I must have sat in the toilet for a long time considering this problem because the attendant eventually knocked on the door to see if I was all right.

"Uhm ..."

"Do you need any help?"

I bet she'll regret asking that until the day she dies.

"Well, actually," I said, opening the door just a little, "if you're offering ..."

I have a snapshot in my head of her crouched on the floor snapping my press studs together as I stood like a toddler being dressed for school.

I tipped her R100. In cringing hindsight, I should have bought her a car.

Your friends don't judge you when these things happen. They think it's cool – or at least they tell you they do. Would I have stopped drinking if someone had sat me down and sternly warned me that I was out of control? That if I didn't stop I would end up hurting myself or someone else? Wouldn't it be great to say yes? That, yes, if I hadn't been part of a group of such enablers, I might have seen the error of my ways?

But I wouldn't have. I would have got new friends. Friends who understood that wherever I went to party, a drink was my 'and partner'. Like a twenty-first. Like my twenty-first.

My twenty-first started off rather sedately. Ten of us went out to eat at a place called Baccarat, which was very posh. Nice-dress-and-heels kind of posh. And we were a pretty eclectic mix: there were journalists, radio and print, and a magazine editor and two accountants. Some lively conversation was had and there was wine, but not too much, and whiskey – just enough – and there was a cake, and in fact if we had all gone home after we had paid the bill that coming-of-age occasion would not have made it into this list at all.

But of course we didn't.

"There's a great house party in Melville," announced one of the print journalists.

"Is that the one with the Angolans?" asked my then flatmate.

"No, that's another one. This is mainly Algerians, I think."

So off we all went, because why turn down a good thing, right? And we ended up somewhere in Westdene and there were indeed Angolans, or Algerians, and lots to drink and smoke if you wanted to and beanbags in the place of chairs and weird trance music playing through the house, and I eventually found myself in the walk-in pantry with a bottle of Jameson, snogging an old boyfriend. And while that part sounds a bit dodgy, it isn't half as dodgy at the part where the police arrived.

The ex and I were blissfully unaware of all this. When we emerged from the pantry, blinking in the brightness of the kitchen's fluorescent lights, we were the only people still there. Well, not the *only* people … There was a man hiding behind the couch. I'm not sure which of us was the more surprised to see the other.

"Who are you?" he demanded.

The ex took charge.

"Never mind that, who are you?"

"I live here."

Well, okay then.

"What happened to your house?" I asked, taking in the overturned bottles and ashtrays.

"It's not my house."

"But you said you lived here?" The ex was in interrogator mode.

"Yes, but it's not my house."

At least that is what he had told the police who had come in on a drug bust apparently. With guns.

"Where is everyone?" I wondered.

"They went with the police, some of them."

I didn't ask if the journey was made willingly.

We had heard nothing, registered nothing. That kitchen cupboard could have doubled as a panic room. I should have suggested it.

Instead we beat a hasty retreat.

"Well, that was fun, wasn't it?" The ex was already planning the story he would write.

I wasn't so sure. But he was right – it did make for a great story. I never did find out whether the revellers were from Angola or Algeria.

The saddest or funniest or creepiest thing, depending on which end of the bar you sit, is that retelling these stories makes me wistful. My head knows I'm better off sober, that stories like these are only supposed to be funny because they all happened so long ago and no one got hurt. Well, almost no one. Sometimes I did, with the odd unexplained bruise or 10 that are the provenance of many alcoholics. We fall down and forget about it, or bang into things or misjudge door handles. We are the active part of an abusive relationship, explaining away our injuries with the same level of denial as that of an abused woman. Except in our case it is us abusing ourselves. If we tell the truth there may be consequences we cannot handle. There may be questions we cannot answer.

But sometimes I miss it. It makes no sense except to other alcoholics or addicts. It's like winning big on a slot machine; there will be one night or one afternoon where everything goes right. You drink just enough to be happy and amusing and not enough to end up face down on the floor of the restaurant bathroom. You get home and go to bed and the next morning you feel fine, no hangover, no desperate phone checking, no listening to the answering machine with bated breath. And you think to yourself, "See? This can be done. I can drink and not fall down and it's lovely." Just like a slots winner might think, "See? Twenty rand and I've won five thousand! Imagine what else I can win!"

But in both cases, that of the gambler and that of the drinker, the odds are stacked against them.

I know that, of course. I've spent every day of the past 14 years reminding myself of that. But there's still a strand of irrational DNA that wishes it were different. That misses the crazy and the confidence and the feeling of slowly going numb and watching lifelong anxiety fading into the distance for a while. Paradise in the bottom of a bottle? For me it was peace. Well, it felt like peace. But, as I was to discover, it was less Winston Churchill's 'peace in our time' and more Neville Chamberlain's policy of appeasement.

CHAPTER 6

Danger

The first time I remember endangering my life while drunk was on Jan Smuts Drive on a Friday night. I don't know how drunk I was, but I knew I shouldn't be driving. And because I knew I shouldn't be driving, my wine-hazed logic was that I should drive as fast as possible so I could get home without blacking out. I remember a booze-fuelled lunch at a pretty street café in Melville where the pizza was good and the service was fast and cheerful. I remember people coming and going throughout the afternoon, staying for a drink or two and then moving on. Some went to other drinking holes, some to do domestic things like fetch children from netball or chess. I also remember thinking how dreadful it would be if I had to do that because it would mean I would have had to stop drinking hours before I actually did.

Lunch ended at around 8 pm. It ended because I realised I could no longer hear properly and I think I was slurring my words and laughing at jokes that I suspect were not funny. It didn't end immediately though, because the café owner came to our table with a bottle of Armagnac and some glasses to tell us he was giving us a brandy on the house because we had the highest bar bill of the day. *The. Highest. Bar bill.* And I was neither embarrassed nor worried. I was very proud. Being able to drink an awful lot means

I must have had an awfully good time. I tossed back a large glass of Armagnac. This was An Achievement.

I don't know who paid the bill. I know it must have been paid because I went to that café many times after that and no one ever said anything about it. And I also couldn't ever ask anyone who was still there at the end of the eight-hour lunch because that would mean admitting that I didn't know. That I had lost time and memory. And I didn't want anyone knowing that. I didn't even want to know that myself.

I do know, though, that I ended up in my car, everything in very sharp focus just for a few minutes. By then I was drunk often enough and hard enough to read the signs. I knew that that clarity wouldn't last long and when it was gone, I would be too and so, it followed, would be the memory of anything I had done. Or not done. I may have briefly considered sleeping it off in the car and perhaps wondered vaguely if there was an undercover parking garage nearby where I could go and park in a top-level corner and shut my eyes for a bit. I knew from experience that the security guards rarely check. I actually knew that. Because I'd actually done that. Even at that point, I never considered that planning how to sleep off a drinking binge undisturbed in a public place might be a sign that I had a problem. Instead I congratulated myself the first time I had thought of it. How very sensible and responsible of me. How very community-minded to prevent myself from being a danger to others. Of course, at that stage it hadn't occurred to me that not drinking at all might be a far better preventative measure. Because why contemplate the impossible?

But I didn't know of any public undercover car parks near Melville, so I decided to drive home. Home was 20 kilometres away. It was a Friday night. It was dangerous. And I knew all this. I also knew I had about 20 minutes – if that – until I didn't know anything any more, until the shutters came down and I ended up on autopilot. That happened sometimes. Sometimes a lot. So I started the engine and pulled away from the curb. First, though, I tipped the car guard R20, a stupid amount of money back in 1997 – a stupid amount of money to tip a car guard even now – but it felt like a tithe. If I paid him a lot, I would get home safely. It made no sense. But, with a thousand-rand bar bill, not much does.

My next memory is of slamming on the brakes behind a minibus taxi. My first feeling was relief that I hadn't had an *actual* accident, so there would be no police or ambulance and I wouldn't be breathalysed. Concern about damaging my car or someone else's, or of hurting myself or someone else, didn't penetrate the alcohol insulator around my brain. I hadn't had an accident. That was all that mattered. I could drive on.

But I couldn't drive on. It was a single-lane road and the taxi was stationary. I watched through my windscreen as the driver's door opened slowly and – just as slowly, it seemed – a man fell out onto the road. I wondered if he was drunk. I was mildly annoyed, but only mildly, because anything more than that would have been too much effort. I wished he would get up and get back in so I could get home, or at least to Rosebank, where there was a mall with a multi-storey car park, before the darkness took over. I didn't have much time.

Suddenly everything sped up. People appeared from the other side of the taxi. One man dropped to his knees and tried to lift the driver. There was a lot of blood. That was when I woke up. Adrenaline does that – it pushes the wine shutters back up. I sat frozen in my car and watched everything go from soft focus to high definition. The man on the ground now looked as though he was wearing a red shirt, the one cradling him was screaming and shouting. Then our eyes met through the windscreen.

"Help, madam!" he shouted. "Please help us!"

It never occurred to me not to.

I unlocked and opened my passenger door and ran to help the helper.

"Let's get him into the car and take him to Rosebank Clinic."

I snapped into high-functioning efficiency. Together we got the driver into the back seat of my car. His friend, the Samaritan, held him up.

The hospital was minutes away, which was lucky because the driver looked as though that might have been all he had left. His eyes were rolling and he was moaning. I remember thinking what a terribly frightening noise it was.

"You are a good woman," wept the other man. "Such a good woman."

No, my friend, I wanted to say, I am a drunk woman. I am a woman who should be calling an ambulance from the safety of my car instead of bundling two strangers, one of whom is bleeding copiously, into my back seat. But I have not been sensible. I no longer remember how to be sensible.

I drove us to the clinic, running every robot. I was terrified that this man would bleed to death. Who would have thought the man had so much blood in him? The weirdness wasn't lost on me. A man could be pumping his last in my back seat and I was quoting *Macbeth* to myself.

I dropped both men at the entrance to the hospital, the friend still thanking me and telling me I was a good woman. He asked God to bless me. I didn't go in. I drove away. I was too afraid to stay. I was too afraid of what would happen to me if I stayed and hospital workers noticed the state I was in. *What* would happen to me? What would happen to *me*? I didn't look back. I drove home, grateful that at that moment, because of the adrenaline, the window of clarity would stay open a lot longer. I was not a good woman. I was a drunk.

But God did bless me. I got home in one piece.

The next morning I woke up feeling the way I usually felt after a good night out, slightly feverish, very nauseous, and with my head feeling as though I'd been pummelled with a hammer. But, as usual, I took it all in my stride – until I got to the bathroom and caught sight of myself in the mirror. I was covered in blood. It was in my hair, on my face and hands and down my top. Of course, I had slept in my clothes. My heart was pounding. What happened? *What happened?* How had I hurt myself? With trembling hands, I felt my head and down my body searching for a wound. I even checked up my nose although I knew there wasn't a chance in hell this could have been a nosebleed. I gapped it back to the bedroom. There was blood on the sheets. But I wasn't hurt, I wasn't in pain. I stripped off with shaking hands – were they shaking because I was frightened or because I was hungover or because I was bleeding? I didn't know. I couldn't find any cuts, or gashes. I wasn't injured, just covered in blood. Which meant something more horrifying. I might have hurt someone else.

I threw up. I didn't make it to the bathroom. I threw up all over my blood-stained sheets. I kept saying to myself over and over again, *It'll be all right, Sam … It'll be all right, Sam.* But louder than that voice was the one in my head saying, *What the fuck have you done this time?* I pulled on a T-shirt and tracksuit pants and made my way down three flights of stairs to the car park.

My car stood innocently in its parking bay in the sunshine. I checked the bumpers back and front. They were undamaged. I broke a sweat with relief and felt it trickle down my back and between my breasts. I sat down on the floor of the carport and cried. I didn't care who saw me. I hadn't hit anything or anyone and that was all that mattered.

But if I didn't hit anyone or anything, how was I covered in blood?

I opened the car door. There was blood everywhere. On the back seat, on the floor. There were even spatters on the gear lever and I noticed for the first time (how I missed it prowling around the car exterior is anyone's guess) the blood on the back windows. And then I remembered. The taxi. The driver. The Samaritan. The hospital. I sank down to the floor again. There was a weird smell. It was making me nauseous. Well, it could have been that that was making me nauseous. It could also have been the eight million glasses of wine and brandy – and, I think, possibly some Kahlúa – from the night before, but I couldn't swear to it. It could be because I had just checked my car to see if I had killed someone and forgotten about it. It could have been all of those things.

I got up and locked the car. Then I went and showered for a long time. I washed the blood out of my hair and off my hands and then I got dressed and went and cleaned the car. It took ages because blood is not easy to remove. Then I showered again. Again, for a long time. I washed more blood out of my hair and off my hands. Then I got out and dried off and had a lie-down. And then I confirmed where I was meeting my friends that night. For drinks.

CHAPTER 7

Understanding

All that differentiates us – young and old, male and female, black and white – are the details. Alcoholism is the most non-discriminating club you'll ever join. It doesn't care who you are or where you come from. It pounces on you and you don't see it coming.

Sometimes it gets you later, long after adolescence and crazy student drinking days. It's like a virus. You can't tell who is carrying it, not unless that person is close to the end of their life, whether it be their drinking life or their physical one. The people in my group were all bruised and confused. We had come to the fire pit by different roads but we were all sitting in the same ash.

I took a friend to an open meeting once. I wanted her to see why I couldn't drink. I wanted to show her how some people in the room had lost their families and their lives and their identities and how, desperate for salvation from themselves, their search had either willingly or unwillingly led them to this room. She was the most resistant of all my friends to the revelation of my problem, my disease, my genetic mutation. Call it anything you want, it's still alcoholism. I thought that if she sat in the same room with friends and relatives of other addicts and heard their stories, she would better understand mine. It would translate better. She could listen to variations on my theme.

But I was wrong. She was utterly shocked that her friend, her successful, wisecracking, loyal, normal friend with a husband and a house and a job, would consider herself in any way on the same page, let alone in the same book as the broken and wounded men and women sitting on uncomfortable plastic chairs in a shabby hall behind a church. I say 'uncomfortable', but it was one of the places I was most comfortable, sitting with comrades and drinking instant coffee out of cracked mugs. She couldn't wait to get out. She almost ran to the car.

"What are you doing here, Sam?" she wept as we faced off over the bonnet. "These people are fucked! They are *fucked*!"

I was speechless. How could she not get it?

"You didn't do those things! You didn't crash your car! You didn't get divorced! You didn't lose your job or drink mouthwash!"

She was crying hard and I cried with her. She cried for me and I cried for her, because she couldn't understand something I thought was so elementary.

"You are not like these people!"

"I am these people!" I found my voice. "There is no difference between me and them, except details!"

She opened the car door.

"I want to get out of here. I don't want to hear this! This isn't you, Sam. It isn't."

She got in and slammed the door.

I stood for a minute. This is what Zev had said. Right at the beginning, right when it all started, this is what he had said.

"This isn't you, Sam."

But it was.

I was like a cracked vase. For years I tried to dress it up by creating more elaborate flower arrangements and then watching them die as the water leaked out. It was only when I joined AA that I realised that if anything was going to survive in it, I had to mend the vase. Bit by bit, a fingernail at a time, a meeting at a time, a share at a time, I clawed my way back from the window ledge of my life and sat there. I searched, hopelessly, for my patient zero, for the place where I caught the disease or whom I caught it from. I found nothing. It just was.

Sometimes it's inside your home before it's inside you. People in and out of group would tell the most hair-raising stories about alcoholic parents or bipolar relationships. I don't know if there's any kind of established link between addiction and bipolar disorder, but there were a lot of people who came from or suffered from it. Sometimes someone would shamble in looking as though they hadn't bathed for a week. Their hands would be shaking and they'd be mumbling. Sometimes they would arrive impeccably dressed, without a hair out of place. And I marvelled again and again at how you never could tell what the skull was like beneath the skin.

I was, I am, what is termed a high-functioning alcoholic. Doesn't that sound good? High-functioning. It gives the impression that even while I pickled my liver, melted my brain and destroyed my nervous system, I was still functioning. And I was. I really was. But that's because I had rules. And I lived by them religiously. I never drank in the mornings. Even at the end, even in those last six months when I knew I was terminal and I couldn't go back, even then, I never drank in the mornings. I never drank at work. Well … that's not strictly true, not *never*. If there was a company function, I would have a beer or a cooler or a glass of wine. But that was it. Gone were the days of the honour bar. I had seen enough people throw up and snog co-workers and fall down at a work party to know I wasn't going to be like them. Those people who couldn't control themselves. Those people who couldn't hold their booze. Those people who embarrassed themselves and had to do the walk of shame into the office the next day and brace themselves for the inevitable side looks and teasing, knowing they'd been the talk of the watercooler that morning. I was right there on the judging panel for that, even knowing that the odds on me going out with friends and hitting the good stuff very hard, after the obligatory drink at the function and the flesh pressing with management were huge. Huge. And, at the end, inevitable.

Because I never drank in the mornings, I also never drank before work. Not alcohol anyway. I would get up about half an hour before I had to so I could drive past the nearest garage shop and pick up a litre of soda water and a can of ginger ale. I'd drink them on the way into work. It's a fantastic combination by the way. Water to take down the swelling in my head and ginger ale to get me started for the day. There's a real zing in Stoney Ginger Beer too. I've often wondered if the manufacturers know how many drinkers use that the following morning? There were loads of us who did. Comparing notes with other drinkers and, for that matter, other addicts, is both comforting and enlightening. It was CS Lewis who said, "Friendship is born in that moment when one person says to another 'What? You too? I thought I was the only one.'"

It's both horrifying and wonderful when you find out how many of you there are.

So I didn't drink before lunch. That would be a sign of being a problem drinker and there was no way I was going to be that.

And lunch had to be with people. I wouldn't dream of going out for lunch and drinking alone or going home and drinking by myself. So if there was no lunch (and by the end I was creating lunches with people I barely knew so I could have a drink), there was no alcohol.

If there was no lunch then there was no drinking allowed before five in the evening. Except on Friday. Everyone starts early on a Friday, don't they? I kept trying to model myself on what other people did. Normal people. Because if I could drink like normal people, then I was a normal person.

I started out as a normal person, I think. When I listened to the stories of strangers in the group, there would be guilt and confusion. As I said earlier, so many had come from broken homes where booze was the go-to girl. They had started their path down the mellow brick road as a form of relief or escape from a violent parent. Sometimes there had been no violence, sometimes just utter neglect. One girl had often waited for hours at school for her mother to come and fetch her, knowing, she said, that the chances were about two out of five that her mum would arrive. She wasn't allowed to catch the bus because apparently it 'wasn't safe'. But, she says, she thinks that's because her mother didn't want to admit that she was incapable of remaining sober long enough during the day to remember to fetch her only child. Giving her a bus pass would be an admission of failure. So this girl, now a grown woman, would wait. And wait. And wait.

One day she decided to walk home. It was quite a long way for a little girl, four or five kilometres, but she had grown uneasy waiting on the street. She never stayed inside the school gates. She didn't want the teachers noticing, and questioning her as to why, day after day, she was the only child left inside. So she walked home. When she reached the gate she saw her mother swaying at the front door.

"What is wrong with you?" she shrieked. "Why didn't you wait for me? I was on my way!"

She had the car keys in her hand.

"I didn't want to stand outside any more," whispered a frightened little girl.

"What are your teachers going to think of me? That I left you alone outside?" Her mother was beyond all reason. "*Never* do that again!"

"What did you do?" I asked her. Children of addicts end up becoming pretty expert liars themselves. They have to be. They are covering for their parents. Protecting their protector, in the hope that they will recover, or at the very least, be kind to them.

"I told her I had extra catch-up lessons every day and I went to the library. And I told her I didn't know what time they would finish because it was different every day. And she believed me and let me have a bus pass. So it got better."

Better? Was that *better*? That your mother admitted in unspoken consent that she was incapable of taking care of you? That you had to be the adult for an adult? She thought so at the time. But she didn't think so now. Because now she was in group with me, chain smoking and trembling. Now she was just like her mother.

Sometimes drinking dulled the pain. Kids who saw their parents anaesthetised used the same means. Who cares if your dad forgets your birthday if you can drink enough to forget it yourself? I had a lot of sympathy for people with damaged backgrounds. At the time, it made more sense to me than people who came from happy homes. I was a lot less tolerant of that. For a full-blown alcoholic, I came to my surrender with a lot of prejudice. I was angry and disappointed and sick with failure. I felt I had no excuse. And no matter how often I audited, and autopsied, and dug into the why and how of how I had gone from a few glasses of wine on a weekend to having to turn down trifle or tiramisu because it smelt so wonderful, I couldn't find a reason for my insatiable need for drink.

I had grown up in a good home. We weren't the Cosbys, but then again, as it turns out, not even the Cosbys were the Cosbys. I don't come from a family of heavy drinkers. My parents had a glass of wine with dinner and sometimes a gin and tonic on the patio or a scotch before bed, but that was it. I really had no interest in drinking when I was younger; I wasn't at all curious about the liquor cabinet – although I did like the smell when my mother drank sherry. And every now and again we were allowed a small glass and it was delicious, but it didn't make me want any more. It was nice and I felt grown-up.

I went to a nice Catholic school and we lived in a nice house and had nice friends and were the most average suburban family you could have imagined. And I was quiet and got better-than-average marks at school, and the most daring thing I did with my friends was to drink a bottle of Cape Velvet liqueur, which one girl had pinched from her dad's bar, while on school tour. I can see why kids drink and smoke in school; there's an instant bond in acts of perceived badness. It's the feeling of all being in it together. It's nice. It's comforting.

Of course, there was Southern Comfort and Appletiser – a nice-girls' drink. Sweet, but with a kick. Perfect for Catholic school. And I was a good Catholic girl. The night before the matric farewell there was a pub crawl. I didn't go. I stayed home and listened to a comedy series on the radio and tidied my room. I had no interest in a debauched night on the town. I saw it as frightening excess, an excuse to lose control and the thought terrified me. I like structure,

I needed it. All anxious people need structure because they can't structure things for their brains, so they have to find a practical way to live within a set of rules in order to keep them safe. Safe. Such a very happy four-letter word.

I don't remember a time in my life that I wasn't anxious. The smallest thing would set me off. A new shirt? I would panic if it was 'scratchy'. I wore skirts until my teen years because trousers felt odd. My shoelaces had to look exactly the same or I would re-lace my shoes and start again. If I wore a jersey over my top, it couldn't cover the cuffs of the sleeves, which had to be perfectly even. I didn't like being touched, except by my closest family members. I had a horror of being sticky or dirty. What simply irritated some children almost drove me mad. "Don't be such a drama queen," was a refrain I heard regularly at home.

I couldn't handle loud noises. I still can't. For many years my parents couldn't take me to a restaurant without a garden area, or I would throw up – every time without fail. I would smell the food and other different aromas, even down to the perfume on the lady at the next table, and hear the sounds from the kitchen and each pot clanging and the people talking at the next table and suddenly I would feel trapped and I would panic. My mother says she knew to run me to the bathroom when she saw sweat break out across my top lip. If there was a garden or a play area, I could go outside and cool down and calm down. Sometimes I couldn't go back inside, and stand outside in the dark and watch everyone inside the restaurant at their tables. Eating and chatting and laughing, and wonder why I was different and why I couldn't be more like them. My younger brothers would bring me the bread basket from the table and I would eat bread in the garden and watch.

School was good. There were rules and you were judged on how well you followed them. And I was a good follower. I never got into trouble. Never. University was the same. While others were throwing up on the library lawns and building floats for Rag week, I was studying in the library. Quiet. Safe. My favourite place was the newspaper room at the William Cullen Library at Wits. It was under the main library and you could go and read back issues of the national and local newspapers stretching back almost a century. I loved history. I read my way from the Union to the Republic, through two world wars and the birth and building of apartheid.

I didn't know, at the time, where this need for safety came from. Twenty-five years later, on my parenting show *Great Expectations*, I did a programme on Sensory Processing Disorder. Twenty-five years later I had an answer. No one knew about SPD when I was little, but it explained everything: why I was so 'intense', why I had such extreme reactions to noise and food and lights and touch. Why I always felt isolated, even when surrounded by friends. Why I needed to take medication for depression and anxiety. Now I knew why I had always felt different. I was different. And it wasn't my fault.

But my drinking was my fault, and it got worse and worse and worse. My blackouts became more frequent and I had made a conscious decision to drink at home so I didn't have to drive. It was the end of days, although I resisted it hard. I tried to modify my drinking – not the quantities I was consuming, but the way I was consuming. But it had to end eventually.

I knew I had to stop drinking six months before I stopped drinking. One morning before work, I stood looking at myself in the bathroom mirror. My skin was dry, my eyes bloodshot, my hands shaking. I was brushing my hair as gently as you would a kitten because my head hurt every time the bristles touched my scalp.

Is this how every morning is going to be for the rest of your life?

The question popped into my head out of nowhere. I stopped brushing and stared at myself. I knew in that moment of horrible, cold clarity that I was on borrowed time. I couldn't get through a day without a drink and, as the old adage goes, one is too many and a thousand aren't enough. I had lost my ability to limit, and I was reminded again of the analogy of the radio where the volume knob snaps off and it's blaring at full blast all the time. I thought about starting each day anxious and guilty. My guilt was built on lies and secrecy. I'd been having an affair with the bottle behind everyone's back and I had to end it. But how?

I called an addiction helpline later that day. I spoke to a very kind lady who listened to my story and then started giving me numbers and addresses for meetings. I put the phone down. I couldn't listen. I couldn't stop. Not yet.

Every drink for the next six months was a drink closer to the end. I hadn't given myself an end date; I couldn't bear to think of it. I kept thinking that it would present itself when the time was right. Sometimes I would wake up with an especially bad hangover, thinking, maybe today. Maybe today will be my last day. Like a dieter who binge eats the day before a diet starts on the ridiculous premise and promise that that will be the last pizza, burger or ice cream for *months*! And that night I would suck down my wine as though I was trying to draw it into my veins for the last time, because tomorrow I wouldn't drink. This would be it. Tomorrow morning would be my last hangover. Ever.

It wasn't. Not for six months.

A buddy I met at Narcotics Anonymous (which I preferred to AA, as it was usually a younger crowd) asked me to explain it to him.

"If you knew you wanted to stop and you were going to stop, why did you keep going?" he asked curiously.

"Wasn't it like that for you?" I asked.

"Hell, no!" he laughed. "I only stopped because I got caught at work."

"You took drugs at work?" I was shocked.

"You didn't drink at work?" he raised an eyebrow.

"No!"

Did he know who he was talking to? I'm a woman who won't drive in the bus lane.

"But didn't you want to stop?" I was curious.

He shrugged.

"Sam, I never thought about stopping. If I thought about anything it was about the next hit, not the last one."

I didn't understand.

"But if it was affecting your work, weren't you worried you would lose your job?"

He smiled.

"I was only worried about when I'd get a gap for another line."

It was a world away.

"But you didn't answer my question," he persisted. "Why did you keep going?"

I thought about it while he went on.

"Because, if the first step to fighting it is supposedly facing it and you'd already faced it, why didn't you fight it? Why didn't you stop that day?"

"I couldn't fight it," I said slowly. "On some level I knew I just had to wait it out."

"Wait what out?"

"Myself."

Two weeks before the end, I decided I would stop drinking until Christmas. Possibly Christmas Eve, but no earlier than that. It was my last battle, the last kicks of the dinosaur before the Ice Age. Maybe, just maybe, if I could stay sober for two and a half weeks, I could break the back of it. Maybe I just needed a long break (at that point, two weeks seemed like an eternity) and that would somehow reset my drinks counter. And maybe it wouldn't be that difficult. I was on leave for a month. It was a happy time of year. I'd get a tan, swim in the pool, eat too much dessert and generally unwind. And I wouldn't need a drink. I might *want* a drink. But I wouldn't *need* one. A holiday would take the same edge off that a glass or six of wine would.

I wanted to lose a few kilograms before Christmas, I told my mother over lunch.

"Really, Sammy?" she said, sipping her wine.

I tried to ignore the lurch in my stomach. It smelled so good. But it was a week into the two and a half weeks so I was nearly halfway there and I could resist. I could. I would.

"Yes, it'll be good for me, especially if Daddy is being all weird about it."

Get that dig in there, Sam. Stuffy old Daddy noticing things he shouldn't.

She ignored the jibe.

"Maybe I should stop for the same time," she wondered. "I've got a couple of kilos to lose."

My mother always thought she had a couple of kilos to lose. She didn't.

"I'll think about it."

I don't know if she did think about it. I do know I thought about it. I thought about it every day. I couldn't stop thinking about it, and that made me very uncomfortable. With every glass I didn't pour the realisation got stronger and stronger that I wasn't in control of the situation at all. I craved – physically craved – a drink. I even dreamed about wine. And that is not normal.

Is this how every morning is going to be for the rest of your life?

That question popped back into my mind time and time again. I didn't want every morning to be like that morning almost six months ago, shivering and shaking and sore in front of the bathroom mirror, but I didn't want every evening to be so boring and cold and stark, the way it felt without a glass of wine or whiskey in my hand. Could I really not have one without the other? What if I just drank on weekends? And Fridays? And once during the week? It was a crazy kind of custody negotiation I carried on with myself. Sober Sam could have Monday to Thursday and Sunday nights (*not* afternoons, in case there was lunch) and she could alternate Wednesday with Drinking Sam. Neither Sam was happy with the arrangement. They both felt that they were losing on the deal.

Then, 10 days into my two and a half weeks of sobriety, I went out to dinner and there was wine. It was the last girls' night out before Christmas and all the usual suspects were there.

"Come on, Sam, just have a glass." Pippa was waving the bottle of Chardonnay at me, all golden and buttery and mouth-watering.

"No thanks, I'm off the sauce until Christmas Day."

There was a loud collective groan. Almost as loud as the solo groan sounding off in my head.

"But why?" asked Sue. "It's Christmas!"

"Well, it's not really Christmas," I said weakly. "Not yet anyway."

Pippa laughed.

"But it *is* Christmas! It's our Christmas dinner for us girls!"

And that was it, right there. That was the loophole. I hadn't had to look for it; Pippa had opened it up and I crawled straight through it.

"And we're not going to see each other again before Christmas so ... Cheers!"

And there was a toast and magically a glass of wine and then one of port and I didn't care what else because that warm wonderful feeling spread through my body like every Christmas, birthday and orgasm rolled into one glorious endorphin experience and ... I was home. And I never ever wanted to leave again. And, in that moment, I knew that any chance of turning back, even the slimmest of the slim, was lost.

CHAPTER 8

First step

The day it all finished started out as a very ordinary day. It was 22 December 2001. Martin and I were going to my parents for a drinks party. I made a dessert and I went over early to help my mum put chips and dips and nuts into bowls. She had a glass of wine on the kitchen counter and, without thinking, I poured myself one. She looked at me curiously.

"You said you weren't going to drink until Christmas Day."

I laughed.

"It's near as dammit."

I don't remember anything else until I got home. I lost six hours. I don't know what happened. Well, I've been told what happened. I've been told that no one realised I was anything more than a little tipsy. I've been told I was the life and soul of the party. I apparently asked the next-door neighbour if he would teach me how to take the top of a champagne bottle off with a sword. I don't know if he agreed.

The next thing I remember is standing in the driveway of my home, my husband in tears in front of me. We were in front of our respective cars.

"Do you know you drove home all the way on the right-hand side of the road?" he demanded.

I didn't.

"Tell me what to do, Sam," he begged. "Tell me what I can do to help you because you are going to kill yourself."

And possibly someone else.

"I can't go on like this," he said, rubbing his eyes. "I can't go on worrying about you. I can't keep fighting you on your drinking. I don't know what to do! Tell me, Sam, because I will do anything. Anything."

And, in that moment, I did know what to do. I knew I had run out of choices.

"Take me to AA."

He stopped.

"What?"

"Take me to AA. I don't know how … I don't care how, but I have to go."

And now I was crying.

"I'm so sorry, darling. I'm so sorry."

And I was so sorry. I was sorry for all the hurt. I was sorry for his sleepless nights and his worry and his frustration, and I was sorry that I'd put our relationship in jeopardy time after time because I couldn't stop doing the one thing he hated above all – getting drunk. And I was sorry that he was in so much pain and that I had caused it all.

And, as much as I was sorry for him, I was sorry for me too. Because it was over. My best friend, my life support, the gas in the tank, the water in the bath, the food on my plate, the peace in my soul – because that's how it felt – had to go. And in that moment I didn't think I could live without it. Or maybe that I could, but not alone.

He took me in his arms.

"It's all right, Sam. It's all right," he soothed. "Let's get you in the house and we'll talk tomorrow … We'll go and get help tomorrow."

I broke away from him.

"No!" I yelled. "It has to be now. It has to be tonight."

He shook his head; he didn't understand. How could he?

"If I don't go tonight, Martin, I will never go. By tomorrow it will be too late."

What would be too late? Why would 12 or 14 or even 24 hours matter? Because it would. Because I might not be this desperate tomorrow. I might decide that today had just been an anomaly, that I hadn't eaten enough or that I'd mixed my drinks or that Martin had overreacted and I hadn't driven home as badly as he'd said I had or that he was just being an over-cautious stick in the mud. And, worse, I might wake up tomorrow feeling okay; the hangover might only be a five-out-of-ten instead of an eight or a nine, and then I would think how silly I had been to worry about it at all.

No. I had to go there and then. While I was watching my marriage teetering on the brink of failure as my husband tried to work out if he could live with a woman who loved something more than she loved him. While I reeked of my own vomit. (Had I been sick in the car or the driveway? I can't remember now and nor can he.) While I was lying bruised and broken on the rocks at the bottom of a wine well of my own creation. There and then. So I couldn't turn back.

"Please, Martin," I sobbed. "It has to be now."

He stood there and looked at me, uncertain. Did he know then that this time it was different? I had cried and apologised before, but I had never asked him for help.

"How do I find them?' he said, bewildered. "Who should I call?"

"Call Pam," I said. "She will know what to do."

Pam was a recovering alcoholic. She had been sober for about eight years at that point. She was a cool alcoholic. She never minded other people drinking near her or around her. She drank more Diet Coke and Snapple than anyone I knew. She smoked like a chimney. She swore enough to ripen fruit. She wasn't some sad, drinking-scotch-out-of-a-paper-bag alcoholic. If you could get an Addict Calendar, she would Miss December for sure.

"Are you sure?" he said. "Are you absolutely sure you want me to do this?"

His unspoken words hung between us. Was I sure I wanted to cross the line between heavy drinker and full-blown alcoholic, with the honesty and the shock and the other consequences of getting clean, with all it would encompass? Was I sure I wanted to come out of a closet, knowing that the door would close swiftly behind me? I don't think either of us back then had a concept of what it would be.

But, yes, I was sure. I was sure this couldn't happen again. And I was tired. I was tired of excuses and hangovers and half-truths and heart palpitations and cold sweats and hand tremors. I was tired of all of it. I didn't know how I would live without drinking. But I knew I couldn't live with it.

"Yes, I'm sure," I said. "Please call her. Please call her now."

And he did. He called her there and then, standing in the driveway next to the car while I slumped down next to the front tyre and cried with relief and sadness and fear. And then he put me in his car and we drove to Pam's house.

Pam's house smelt of vanilla, I'll never forget that. She was all business-as-usual, very efficient was Pam.

"There's an open meeting up the road in an hour," she said. "So we'll have something to eat and then go. Sam, have you eaten?"

"No, she hasn't," Martin told her.

I didn't know whether I had or I hadn't.

"Could you eat something? Because I think you should."

She eyed me doubtfully. I was used to those looks from lots of people. The 'what will she do next?' look.

"I don't know."

I ate rice. Pam's husband, Bruce ordered Chinese takeaways and I ate rice. Everything felt as if it was in slow motion and maybe it was.

Bruce was very good to Martin.

"It'll be okay," he said. "AA will help, it really will. You can go as well if you want, at least to the open meetings. Or they've got a group for family members as well."

"Shall I come with you tonight?" Martin asked.

"No."

I didn't have to think about it. This was not a road I could share. I had to close this door firmly on my own. Anyone else's help would dilute my own resolve. I didn't want to wake up the next day and wonder if I had taken this step alone or because someone had helped me. And I knew I would latch on to that as an excuse the next time a glass of wine presented itself. That little voice would say, "You see, Sam, you only did it for him. You don't really want to stop, not when it makes you so happy."

I couldn't leave any loopholes.

Pam gave me a clean T-shirt.

"Would you like to shower before we go?" she asked.

"No, I'm okay," I said, thinking that I would never be okay again.

She exchanged glances with Bruce.

"Sam, you have puke in your hair."

It was difficult to laugh at that one, but somehow I managed.

"I don't think anyone will notice."

I really didn't. I hadn't noticed. How would anyone else?

And so Pam and I sat in a crowded municipal hall, me in a clean T-shirt with vomit in my hair, and I listened and cried. I looked around and everyone there seemed so together. From the smartly dressed young guys to the older, more grizzled members. I kept thinking, all these people drink like me. And I have nothing else in common with any of them.

I didn't say anything that night. Other people spoke up about how they felt and what they thought about attempting and managing their sobriety over a traditionally very boozy season. I thought about how a normal person would have waited until after Christmas Week, otherwise known as Extreme Drinking Week, to stop imbibing. And then I remembered that I wasn't normal. I was one of them. I was them.

Pam collected all the leaflets and bought me a little copy of the AA's Big Book, which became my bible of sobriety. I sat in the car on the way back to her house clutching them like some form of lifesaving medication. I hoped they would carry some magic spell I could just keep repeating. By then I had sobered up enough to smell the vomit. And, as usual, I was embarrassed and ashamed. But tonight I was something else as well. I was relieved.

"Sorry, Pam. I'm sorry I ruined your evening."

Let's start with what I'm used to, apologising. The new stuff can come later.

"I'm not."

I must have misheard.

"You're not what?"

"I'm not sorry Martin called me. And you didn't ruin my evening. In fact, I'm glad this happened."

Pam glanced over at me.

"Sam, I haven't had a drink in eight years. And I'm open about it."

"Yeah, I know. I'm really impressed. I don't know how you do it."

"I do it by keeping myself hyper-aware. I make sure that, if I start feeling frustrated or wanting to let off steam, I recognise that as a trigger and I go and do something else."

She kept driving.

"But the problem is that it becomes habit. For you and for everyone else. So some people don't think I'm a real alcoholic because I've been sober for so long. And they ask if I'm sure I couldn't just have one drink and see."

I could understand that. I think a part of me at that point still believed that if I could put enough time between this last drink and the next one in, say, a decade's time, I would have reset the switch. Taken myself back to factory settings.

"So how does that make you glad you're sitting next to a woman with puke in her hair stinking up your car?"

She pulled over to the side of the road and turned off the ignition.

"Because every now and again I get complacent. I wonder if they're right. I stopped drinking when I was a lot younger and maybe it was just a phase. Maybe I was overreacting and being dramatic."

I watched her; she was staring unblinking ahead of her, beyond the windscreen. And she was quiet for a moment. And then she turned to face me.

"And then you called. Or rather Martin called. And you arrived at my house in vomit clothes and off-your-face drunk. And you

71

reminded me of how it was for me – not just every now and again, but all the time."

"Okay?"

I was still not seeing how this was a good thing.

"And instead of being grossed out like I probably should have been …" There was a pause. "… I was jealous."

I woke up properly then.

"*What?* Why? Why would you be jealous of … of … of this!" I gestured to myself. Sad and smelly, with my eye make-up everywhere.

"Because, Sam, I remember how good it was to have those first few glasses of wine. I remember the confidence and the fun. And even though it pretty much always ended like this … I dreamed of some kind of magic way of making sure it wouldn't. But there isn't one."

We sat in silence for a few seconds.

Then I said, "I wish there was one."

She took my hand.

"Me too."

Then she said again, "But there isn't one. And thank you for coming over tonight and reminding me of that."

"In the most warped way possible … you're welcome."

She squeezed my hand and then turned the car back on.

"And now we tell your parents."

"*What?*"

I had never thought about that. I was 28. Who still tells their parents everything at 28? And yet she was right. My father had noticed a change in my drinking patterns at roughly the same time I'd started my own long and painful journey of honesty, that Mirror-Mirror-On-The-Wall moment in my bathroom, when I'd had to accept that denial was not just a river in Egypt. He hadn't said anything to me, but he had said something to my mother. And she told me. Over a glass of wine.

"Daddy is a bit worried about your drinking, Sammy."

I smarted. That was my usual response when someone got 'a bit worried' about my drinking. My first line of defence had always been offence.

72

"What's wrong with him?" I bristled.

See what I did there? See whose fault it was?

"He says you used to drink a glass or two of wine when you came over and now you're on three or four."

"So what?"

She blinked at that.

"Well … I don't know."

Silence.

"Do you think you're drinking more than normal, darling?"

Normal. Even in my darkest moments I found humour. How else do we go on? Was I drinking more? Well, more than what? More than last week when it was a case of wine and two bottles of bourbon, one of which I had been given as a thank-you present at work and, boy oh boy, were they welcome! More than the man next door who could lop the top off a champagne bottle with a sword?

More than my friend Sue who was definitely my partner in crime – or, rather, my partner in wine? I told her about that exchange.

"Well, your parents do have really small wineglasses," she said comfortingly, pouring some more into a substantially bigger glass. More than her?

Yes, probably.

"No, I don't think so," I said, pretending to think about it.

Now I had to tell her that I did think so.

I think it was Pam who called my parents. I can't remember, and neither could they. But I do remember sitting on the sofa telling them I had just come from an AA meeting and I could never drink again.

My father sat and listened. My mother sat and cried.

"But, Sammy, you aren't drinking that much, are you?"

I nodded.

"I am, Mom. Today was proof."

"But it was a party, and you were only a bit tipsy."

Tipsy enough to drive home American style.

"I think you're being a bit dramatic, darling, I really do."

Pam stepped in.

"She's an alcoholic, Mary; I've seen it. And she needs you to accept it if you're going to help her stay sober."

My mother just looked at me with tears in her eyes. Her love for her kids was shamelessly subjective. We were all amazing in her eyes. It was beyond her capabilities to look at her nerdy, quiet, overachiever daughter and hear that she was a few shots away from sucking sherry out of a paper bag.

My father didn't say much that night. He just thanked Pam for bringing me over.

I hugged Mommy goodbye. I told her I was sorry for being such a profound disappointment. I was sick with guilt. She was so proud of me. What would she be proud of now? She hugged me back hard and whispered fiercely that she thought I was being silly, that I would never be a disappointment.

She was so small and soft and she smelled so sweet and safe. I wanted to stay there in her arms for hours and have her tell me everything was going to be all right and then tuck me into bed and give me a cup of warm Oros. Because that's what she would do when I was little: heat it up. But I was big now. So she couldn't.

Back we went to Pam's house. I was tired now and everything was starting to hurt; even my fingernails hurt – and they were plastic, so technically they weren't even mine, but they still hurt.

Pam gave me the leftover Chinese and Martin drove me home.

And I never drank again.

The next week I started to eat.

PART 2

Eating

CHAPTER 9

Mirror, mirror, on the wall ...

What does it feel like, shifting from one side of the mirror to the other? Peering out at others rather than in at the self. It's hard to describe. The best analogy I can think of is that of getting sunburned. You're on the same beach as everyone else, under the same sun as everyone else, and you put on sunscreen like everyone else, but there's no factor high enough to protect you. You don't know that when you lather it on, of course. You tell yourself it will be enough, as it will for everyone else.

And then you fall sleep on the sand. And when you wake up you are burnt and you have a fever. Everyone else seems fine. They are splashing in the waves and strolling down the beach and you cannot move. Everything is on fire.

When you go home, you have a cold bath. You take an anti-inflammatory. You tell yourself you will never go in the sun again. You know it's dangerous. But the next day the sky is so blue and the sand is so white and the sea is so calm, it invites you back. And if other people are playing in the water, why can't *you*? And so you do, the pain of the previous day a distant memory. And in a cool breeze you can't feel the sun doing its work as diligently as it did yesterday. And the result this time is second-degree burns and a higher fever. And all the time, the damage is sinking deeper and deeper below the surface of your skin and you don't see it.

And one day – and sometimes you don't see it coming and sometimes you've seen it coming for a while but only as a threat – you find out that you can't go to the beach during the day any more. That even to spend an hour in the waves in the heat of the day might kill you. That you can go in the morning or the evening if you wear a big hat and total blockout on your face and are covered from head to toe, but at no other time and in no other way. And you have to accept that. And you look at the other people on the sand and you wonder how and why you got like that and they didn't, and the hardest part is making peace with never knowing the answer. You were just different. That is all.

What nobody tells you about getting sober is how much it's like calling an end to a destructive relationship. One where you just know you need to get out or you'll be ruined for the next guy, but you still love the first one. And that you will never, ever get over it.

That first feeling is one of relief. It's very strange. I was not sure how I would live without it, but I did know I could no longer live with it. The morning after I stopped drinking, I felt free. I thought about all the things I wouldn't have to worry about any more. I wouldn't have to look at my phone first thing in the morning to check who I had called. I wouldn't have to worry that I had made some grand promise to someone I wasn't going to be able to fulfil. Gone were hangovers and hand tremors. I would get better. I would be able to see the whites of my eyes. By the end of it all, I wasn't looking at life through rose-tinted glasses, more like rose tinted sclera. That wouldn't happen now. I wouldn't wake up ten times a night needing water and/or the toilet. I would sleep through. I would eat three times a day instead of once or twice. I might even exercise for fun and not to combat the effects of the night before. I would wake up clearheaded! I would spend less on painkillers! I would spend less full stop! The booze bill was thousands every month by then. I was almost excited by the thought. And I would be safe. 'Safe' was a word that cropped up in almost every thought. I would be safe when I drove. Safe when I was out with friends. Safe while I slept. It was a feeling more than a thought, and looking back that was good, because I think that if I had realised back then that I would never be safe again, I would have rolled over with a bottle of sherry and died.

By the time I called it quits on drinking, the physical effects were undeniable. Every morning I would wake up with my head throbbing. Every single day I had a headache. It sounds like an exaggeration, but it really isn't. I'd move through the house getting ready for work, being careful not to make any sudden movements that would send my brain slamming against the inside of my skull. My heart would beat as though it was jumping out of my chest; my mouth would be so dry it felt as though it was stuffed with paper towel. I had developed a permanent hand tremor and people had started to notice. I lied about it of course. I told them it ran in the family and that my father had it as well. It never ceased to amaze me how easily that explanation was accepted. People accept the lies of the secret drinker because it is all you lie about. My father did have a tremor but his was due to a childhood illness, certainly not hereditary. Half the truth was better than no truth at all.

I was drinking at least three litres of water a day by then too, and yet I remained thirsty. I chewed gum a lot just to keep the saliva glands working. I was tired all the time, but I never missed work for a hangover – I never missed work at all. In fact, on a list of 20 AA questions for you to ask yourself if you're wondering whether you're an alcoholic (which, in my opinion, is enough to confirm that you probably are), I ticked all but five, and all of them had to do with work. No, I had never missed work; no, it hadn't affected my efficiency; no, I hadn't got myself into financial difficulties; no, I had never been treated by a doctor for it; and, no, I had never been hospitalised or institutionalised because of my drinking. But 15 out of 20 wasn't great odds on turning the clock back, particularly as the premise was, and is, that if you answer yes to one of the questions there's a possibility you might be an alcoholic, to two and there's a distinct chance you are, and to three or more you are. Like, for real, you are. And I had ticked yes to 15. Always the overachiever.

Why didn't I go to rehab? I still get asked that. I certainly qualified. But the short answer is that I didn't go because I was afraid. I was afraid that I would dry out in a secure institutionalised environment and then be unable to sustain it when I was back in my own world. I didn't want to be protected, to have someone watching my every move and policing what I ate and drank. I didn't want to get used to that. I was certain that I had to learn to function again as a sober person in my own world.

The first and most immediate issue was physical. Three days after I stopped drinking, my hair, which had always been dry and flyaway, started lying heavy and oily against my head. I went from washing it every other day to washing it every day and sometimes twice a day. My skin was much the same, and I ended up using a face wash for teenage boys to try to deal with the same skin eruptions that tend to plague them. My poor body had spent years battling dehydration and now it was getting its own back in spades. My hands were clammy all the time and even in the heat of summer I was consistently cold. It took almost six months for everything to regulate. By that time the whites of my eyes were exactly that: white. My nails and hair had stopped chipping and breaking respectively and I was almost a new woman.

But long before that happened I drove myself mad asking, so now what? Naively I thought that I could go back to living a normal life, like normal people. But I had been drinking heavily for almost a decade; I no longer knew what normal was, certainly not on a day-to-day, hour-by-hour basis. At one of the meetings that year, someone had referenced a psychologist who said that you press pause on your emotional development as a person from the moment you cross over into addiction. Even allowing for a couple of years of 'vaguely normal', that was eight years on pause. I was going to have to learn how to function from the emotional age of 20.

Two days after I quit, I had my first hallucination. I was standing in Pick n Pay with a trolley of vegetables when I noticed something moving in a bag of potatoes. I stopped and watched it, thinking at first that it was an insect that had somehow got in between my bagging them and weighing them, but as I continued to watch, the movement stopped. And then started again in the apples. Now something was moving in two bags. I watched the potatoes and the movement stopped, but out of the corner of my eye I saw it start in the bananas. I watched the bananas, but when they stopped moving, the potatoes started up again. I broke into a sweat. Was I going mad? How would I know? Does a mad person know when he or she is going mad? I left the trolley in the middle of the shopping aisle and made my way back to my car where I sat trembling and crying, waiting for my hands to stop shaking enough to allow me to drive home. I had spent two days sweating and shivering and shaking; I'd had a pounding headache as well, but I knew that that was withdrawal and I'd accepted it. It couldn't go on forever. But this was new. No one had told me I would begin fearing the movement of fruit. When I got home I phoned Pam.

"You need to see a psychiatrist," she said worriedly.

Oh dear.

"Why?"

"Because this is withdrawal and you need medication to get through it."

"Won't it go away on its own?" I asked weakly.

Please let it go away on its own.

"It should, but please make an appointment urgently."

She gave me some names. I chose to call the doctor at the hospital furthest away. Coincidentally, she was the one who specialised in addiction, but I didn't know that at the time. All I could think of was that it was unlikely I would bump into someone I knew in a psychiatrist's office across town. Because – the horror – what if some actually found out?

I sat in her rooms reading pamphlets on bipolar mood disorder and waiting to see if I had done some irreparable brain damage.

Her response when I told her about the jumping fruit was one of concern.

"You should have been on Librium!" she said.

81

That sounded both exciting and scary. It meant that there was a Real Problem, and therefore an Actual Solution.

"What's that?" I said, trying not to sound too eager.

"It's a benzodiazepine."

Alrighty then.

She pulled a huge book from her bookcase.

"It'll ease the symptoms of withdrawal."

"Meaning that moving vegetables are a symptom of withdrawal?" I tried to make a joke.

She didn't laugh.

"Meaning that seeing things moving that aren't moving is a symptom of withdrawal."

Tough crowd.

She gave me a prescription for meds that would calm me down (yay), stop me seeing double and trembling (double yay) and bring me back to earth (yay?).

One of the drugs was a benzodiazepine called Xanor. I had no idea what it was at the time, but I dutifully started taking it that day. After two days I flushed it all away, every pill. It was wonderful. It 'took the edge off'. It made my life seem quieter and sanded down all the sharp edges. It had exactly the same effect as alcohol. I couldn't risk it. I couldn't afford to fall down or fall back; I couldn't afford to swap one addiction for another. So, delicious and wonderful and promising as it was, the Xanor had to go. And it did. And, anyway, the hallucinations stopped after a few days. I would be fine.

But I wasn't fine. Actor Christian Slater once said, "Work is my hobby, staying sober is my job." As the days passed, first one day then two days, a week, then two, it became increasingly apparent that I was treading water in the dark, desperately trying to stay afloat in the middle of an ocean with very big waves and no land in sight.

I didn't know how to live without a drink. Beyond the physical withdrawal was the bewilderment about how I had got to this point, anxiety mixed with grief; I was alone and my support structure was gone. As much as my family and friends tried to understand, it was like trying to talk to them across eight rugby fields. I didn't have the words to explain how desperate I felt each day – despite my new-found clearheaded-ness in the mornings, despite the relief every time I turned on the car that the odds were in my, and everyone else's favour that I wouldn't have an accident. It was a lonely time.

AA helped. It did more than help – for that first year it kept me alive. It taught me how to walk again after a long time as an emotional cripple. When people talk about staying sober for a month, like 'Ocsober', they talk about 'giving up'. It's a sacrifice. It's the same with smokers; they 'give up' smoking when they stop. I have yet to meet a smoker who has 'stopped', until a very long time after their last cigarette. It takes a long time to reposition your thought process to seeing 'giving up' less as an act of deprivation and more as a surrender to a force greater than you. Step One of the 12 Steps, which are the bedrock of sobriety, is: "We admitted we were powerless over alcohol – that our lives had become unmanageable." And that's the best and most elegant way of putting it.

1. *We admitted we were powerless over alcohol – that our lives had become unmanageable.*
2. *Came to believe that a Power greater than ourselves could restore us to sanity.*
3. *Made a decision to turn our will and our lives over to the care of God as we understood Him.*
4. *Made a searching and fearless moral inventory of ourselves.*
5. *Admitted to God, to ourselves and to another human being the exact nature of our wrongs.*
6. *Were entirely ready to have God remove all these defects of character.*
7. *Humbly asked Him to remove our shortcomings.*
8. *Made a list of all persons we had harmed, and became willing to make amends to them all.*
9. *Made direct amends to such people wherever possible, except when to do so would injure them or others.*

10. *Continued to take personal inventory and when we were wrong promptly admitted it.*
11. *Sought through prayer and meditation to improve our conscious contact with God as we understood Him, praying only for knowledge of His will for us and the power to carry that out.*
12. *Having had a spiritual awakening as the result of these steps, we tried to carry this message to alcoholics and to practise these principles in all our affairs.*

I showed a friend my copy of the 12 steps once and she said it seemed very strict and how did I feel about how Christian it was? I couldn't answer her. How do you look at someone you love, who loves you back and is desperate to support you, and scream, "You stupid bitch, don't you get it? The only way to do this is in black and white! There's no room for grey. There's no leeway!" You can't. I couldn't. She wasn't being dismissive. She just didn't understand, although she tried. The God of the 12 Steps is not a forgiving God. He is a stern God, the God of my childhood spent at Catholic school in varying degrees of guilt. And I needed that. I still need that.

I am a Christian, but that was incidental. Alcohol had power over me completely. If there was a higher, stronger power than that it could only be God and I relied on that, first with desperation and then with relief, and eventually with acceptance. I prayed every day, over and over, for help and release. I felt like that lonely voice crying in the wilderness, the one from Psalm 13: "How long will you forget me, O Lord? Forever?" There was no booming voice in response. No burning bush. No lights in the sky. But with every day I was sober, I felt Him. "Be still and know that I am God." And I was. And I did. And as the days became weeks and the weeks became months, I trusted the process more and more. I had to. The alternative was unthinkable.

I had to accept that there was no alternative route. There are no back roads. There are no short cuts. AA is not a satellite navigation system looking for the best way through the traffic.

There is only one way. You are only allowed to travel one road. And sometimes there will be a *lot* of traffic on that road. And I had to learn to navigate it, every broken traffic light, every roadblock, and especially, every unexpected pothole. And there were many. Like lunch.

One of the many things you don't think about is how you will get from one end of the day to the other. It sounds simple, to wake up, have a shower, eat breakfast, go to work, come home, eat dinner, go to bed. Easy, hey? Not for a newly sober person, it's not. One of the AA tenets is *Just for one day*. For me, sometimes a day was an eternity, and never more so than when a situation popped up that I had only ever associated with drinking. As I say, like lunch.

I couldn't go out to lunch any more; I didn't know what I would do. How would I get through a whole meal without wine? Like a smoker who is trying to stop smoking and can't work out what to do with his or her hands, I didn't feel comfortable without a glass in my hand in a social setting.

I was invited to a wedding in the first month of my sobriety. I left after an hour, having drunk three glasses of orange juice. Cold drink was no substitute. You couldn't nurse a Coke. For a start, it came in the wrong glass. My fingers were used to curling around the familiar bowl of a wine glass, not clutching a hollowed-out highball. A soft drink was awful once it was warm, whereas wine was the embodiment of eternal youth, nectar at any and all temperatures: cold for a Sauvignon Blanc on a hot summer's day, warm like glühwein or Irish Coffee in winter, and room temperature for all other times. It also had undisputed medicinal properties ... How many times have you heard that a hot toddy chases away a cold? How can anything made of whiskey, honey and spice be anything but glorious? I tried that a lot while I was sick actually and to this day I'm not sure whether it actually does cure a cold or just makes you so drunk you forget that you have one.

Sober, I also turned down a weekend away at the Vaal. That was the first time someone got angry with me – and the first incident that separated my friends from my drinking partners. Drinking partners, and there were many, took this new-found need for sobriety as a cry for attention or a Sam-being-dramatic phase. I wasn't an alcoholic. I was just a heavy drinker and if I was that worried, I could just scale back, couldn't I?

"You're seriously not coming?" Tara asked indignantly.

"I'm seriously not coming."

"But why? It's going to be amazing! And James and Bridget are coming!"

Because James and Bridget coming or going was going to be the deciding kicker on whether or not I could stay dry in the face of a whole lot of lovely champagne wetness.

"I can't, I really can't. I can't come and not drink."

Tara clicked her tongue in annoyance.

"Of course you can! Or you can just have one or two. I'll even stop you if you want!"

One or two. Darling, if I could just have one or two I wouldn't be here, chewing the sides of my nails and sweating and shaking and drowning in embarrassment and anxiety instead of in Merlot. And the thought that she could stop me, that anyone could stop me, what a laugh! My husband hadn't stopped me, a permanent hand tremor hadn't stopped me, enough lost memories to fill Kimberley's Big Hole hadn't stopped me. How did she, with a glass of champagne in hand and prawns on the braai, think that by saying, "Sam, that's enough," she would succeed where bigger and stronger and, frankly, more convincing arguments had failed?

"Well, to be honest, I think that's really selfish – everyone's expecting you."

And, to be honest, I couldn't give two fucks, because sobriety was first, second and third here in terms of importance. And I knew there wasn't a chance I could sit in a room or on a deck with free-flowing wine and drink water. I couldn't. I wished, one of many million wishes, that I could. But I couldn't.

After a while, I stopped seeing Tara. I told myself it was because she lived a long way away and the drive was tedious. But it wasn't that. It was because I couldn't see the point of travelling anywhere to see someone with whom I had nothing in common but happy inebriation. I'm still not sure whether I was a casualty of her war or she of mine.

I did think she was monumentally unfair. In the early days, I thought anyone who didn't understand or want to understand, was monumentally unfair. You were either with me or you were against me – it was that simple. With many years of hindsight, I can see that I was the one who was unfair. For someone who doesn't have a drinking problem, it's a foreign concept to think someone else incapable of moderation. Isn't it just a matter of willpower? Why not just cut down? I had no time for them, because I knew I couldn't 'just cut down'. To expect someone who wasn't in that realm to understand only showed my lack of understanding and my intolerance. But I was new at sobriety then. To be asked to drink moderately was like being asked to breathe only occasionally. It's such a foreign concept for most people that it was like expecting an English speaker to suddenly be effortlessly proficient in another language. Impossible.

Okay, so back to lunch ... Weddings and weekends away weren't regular occurrences, but lunch was. And dinner. And I couldn't go. I couldn't risk it. I'd rather stay at home. I was safe at home. The day after I stopped drinking, Martin packed all the alcohol in the house into boxes and took it around to my parents. I now lived in a booze-free zone. There was no way that lunch would ever be a booze-free zone. Or dinner. Or a braai at someone else's house to watch the rugby/cricket/sports in general, so I didn't do that either. I became a suburban hermit. I'd resigned myself to never seeing anyone again except by accident, possibly over the now-not-moving vegetables in the supermarket. One by one, my drinking partners dropped off. And my friends – who, it became clear, were the minority partners in my previous life – didn't know what to suggest.

Except one.

"Breakfast," announced Cindy. Cindy and I worked together in the old days at Highveld Stereo. She was on the traffic desk, I was on *The Rude Awakening*. The irony of the show's name does not escape me.

"What?"

"We are going out for breakfast on Saturday."

I blinked.

"Pardon?"

"Well, it makes sense if you think about it."

I didn't know what to think about it.

"Breakfast is the only meal you didn't drink at."

That was true.

"So you can go out for breakfast and it'll feel okay. And you can just drink lots of coffee instead."

She was so confident in her rightness. I took confidence from that. She was eight years younger than me chronologically, but streets ahead in emotional intelligence. Or just far enough away to be objective.

"So we will just go out for breakfast every week. Okay?"

She was right. We went out to breakfast every Saturday for a year. We drank coffee and ate eggs and laughed, and sometimes I cried and, slowly, I learned to make my way back into a social environment. And it was okay.

But lunch and dinner remained verboten for almost a year. I could barely function in a restaurant. Wherever I went, I was sure I could smell wine. My ears were on the same frequency as corks being released from bottles and beer bottles being opened. And I had a glass of ... water. I was bored and restless. Was everything this mundane without a drink? A friend said once that I was more interesting when I was drinking. I told her she was also more interesting when I was drinking. Yet another dinner cut short.

Most invitations I could and would turn down, but you can't turn down your parents. My younger brother Simon had flown out as a surprise for my father's sixtieth birthday and we went out for a nice family dinner. Is there any other kind? It hadn't been a month yet, not a whole month. I got sober on 22 December; it was 18 January. We went to a proper steak restaurant, the kind with sawdust on the floor and expensive meat, overpriced because it had been aged and hung and massaged and whatever else they do to it. Every table had snowy white napkins and shiny knives and forks and ... enormous wine glasses. They were so big that, with the addition of some shiny pebbles and a dahlia head, they could have passed for novelty vases. I felt like a dog that has just found a plate of sandwiches on a side table. He knows he shouldn't eat them, but they are *there*, right there under his nose! What else is he supposed to do? And yet he knows the punishment will be dire so he pauses, trembling, torn between *I can't* and *I must*. And those glasses, so clean and shiny and empty, were standing there willing to be filled with wine. And I paused, trembling, feeling exactly like that. I felt so desperate I couldn't concentrate. My mother, who was in her own private hell about my recent revelation, tried very hard to stay bright and cheerful. My twitching unease wasn't helping. I made it through starters and most of the main course, my temples throbbing, and then she pushed her wine glass a few inches towards me.

"Could you top me up, Sammy?" she said.

Such an innocuous, innocent question. Any other time, I probably wouldn't have registered. But that night I was cold with fury and hurt. It felt like a slap in the face. I know you've chosen not to have any, she seemed to be saying, but I haven't, so please give me more. I knew she thought my recent revelation was overly dramatic. I knew she didn't want it to be true – what mother wants an admitted addict as a daughter? But I couldn't waste time convincing her. And I certainly couldn't hold a bottle of wine in my hand 26 days after I stopped drinking.

"Simon can do it," I said, shoving the glass towards him, and I got up so quickly that my chair fell backwards. Out of the corner of my eye, I saw a waiter stop it falling and, as I ran to the bathroom in tears, he was picking up my napkin and folding it into some aesthetically pleasing shape. I sat on the floor of the toilet with my knees drawn up to my chest, gently banging the back of my head against the wall tiles until I felt calmer. And after 15 minutes I felt well enough to make my way back to the dining room.

I got back to an inevitable atmosphere. My mother was being her glitteriest self, my brother was charming and my father had that set look that men get when they are stoically outlasting an unpleasant situation. The whole picture of the happy family was skew in the frame. And after a few minutes my mother excused herself and, with tears in her eyes, went to the bathroom. What was wrong with her? I hadn't been rude. I didn't think I had anyway. And I was sober, so I was probably right. This wasn't a round of the old game 'Guess by today's reaction what last night's action was'.

"Well, this isn't the best birthday you've ever had, is it?" I said to my father with forced cheer.

"No. No, it's not." He sat back in his chair. "It's not the worst one I've ever had either."

I wondered what the worst one he'd ever had could be. This seemed pretty bad.

Simon went to find my mother, leaving my father and me at the table.

We sat in silence for a minute. But only a minute. I'm not good at silence. I think it's an English thing; we don't like gaps in conversation. Silence makes us awkward.

"Sorry, Daddy."

"It's all right, Sam," he said and patted my hand. "You just concentrate on what you need to do and we'll get by."

Silence again. But companionable silence.

Later that night I took Simon for a drive and asked him what had happened.

"What was wrong with Mommy? Why was she so upset?"

"Well, at first she was upset because she thought you were being a drama queen."

Well, thanks, Captain Obvious.

"So what did you say?"

"I told her you might be, but not about this. I told her you had a drinking problem and that I'd known it since you came to visit in London."

Thank God he didn't know about Nick and the dustbin and the police.

"And I told her to watch your eyes when you got back and count how many times you looked at her glass of wine in a minute."

"And?"

"Well, I was timing and you'd hit about 30 before the minute was up. And then she knew."

He stretched out in the car.

"It's hard for her, Sam."

"It's hard for me too."

"Yes, but you just have to be you. She has to watch."

And he was right. Addiction, like cancer, is a terrible spectator sport.

So now lunch and dinner were off my calendar. But only socially. Because now lunch and dinner were definitely 'in' at my house. Towards the end, I had swapped drink for food many times. Why bother to cook something when you could sit on the sofa with a bottle of something and let that fill you up? I got around to eating once, or sometimes, on a good day, twice, and I wasn't eating much. I'd lost all interest in preparing food; my husband worked late most nights anyway, so it would only be for me. Why bother? As the other kitchen equipment gathered dust, only the bottle opener remained shiny clean.

Now it had to be the other way around.

And that's where my new addiction started. That's when I started to put on weight. Now, instead of eating to live, I would live to eat. It wasn't a conscious decision. It wasn't a decision at all. It started as a method of combatting the need to drink. It didn't present as three meals a day, though; it presented as eating as much ice cream as I could manage. Yes. Ice cream. I'm not the only alcoholic who turned to ice cream. I know of at least three others. One man couldn't go home without eating a Magnum Classic. It had to be the Classic, and if the shop he stopped at to buy one didn't have the Classic, he would leave and go somewhere else. Why ice cream? We don't know. If there are any researchers or medical students out there who like a challenge, feel free to take it on. Maybe because it's high in sugar, like alcohol. Maybe because the combination of sugar and fat satisfies some other, baser need for satisfaction. Maybe the cold as well, an association with ice cubes in a drink. I don't know, I'm no expert. All I knew back then was that it filled the void a little, in a way a salad or a sandwich or a bowl of pasta did not. It filled the gap in more ways than one, unfortunately, because in much the same way I couldn't drink moderately, it seemed I couldn't eat moderately either. Well, not ice cream anyway.

I called Pam.

"I'm eating a lot of ice cream. Is that normal?"

"Well, how much is a lot?"

"A *lot*."

"More than a bowl at a time?"

I wasn't eating it out of a bowl.

"Quite a bit more."

"*How much?*"

"Sometimes a litre."

She hmmmed.

"Well, if it's helping keep you sober, that's not too bad every now and again."

"Yeah … it's only happening every now and again."

"That's okay then."

"The rest of the time it's two litres."

Silence.

"Are you serious?"

I knew that would happen.

"Don't get all judgey."

"I'm not judging. I'm trying to work out what you're eating. How many times a week are you eating ice cream?"

"Sometimes seven."

"What?"

"Sometimes more."

She exhaled deeply.

"I think maybe you should see a dietician."

I didn't see a dietician, because I didn't think it would help. It's not like I didn't know that eating almost my own bodyweight in ice cream was A Bad Thing. I just couldn't afford the alternative. And while I was eating cold, sugary junk food, I couldn't think about drinking. And that was my priority. Yes, I had flushed the prescription tranquiliser, but I had found a new one, one that was freely available and in a variety of different flavours and colours. And sometimes with chocolate bits in it.

I've seen smokers put on weight when they stop smoking. Apparently, you actually burn calories when you smoke and nicotine is a mild appetite suppressant, so it's normal (there's that word again) to put on a little weight when you quit smoking. I was never a smoker, so I had nothing to blame my ballooning weight on but myself. And ballooning is actually an exaggeration. The weight went up, but it was a slow, steady climb. Inner-circle friends who knew my story couldn't understand it.

"I thought you were supposed to lose weight when you stopped drinking," said Anna.

"Yes, you are, but only if you were also eating while you were drinking. I was only drinking."

"So you've just got to eat—"

I stopped her mid-sentence.

"Don't say it. Don't say 'everything in moderation'."

She looked at me curiously.

"But that's what you'll have to do."

But I couldn't.

I tried to add some of the more basic food groups. I managed the odd vegetable here and there, some fruit as well. But I lived and died each day in sugar and carbohydrate cotton wool. The feeling of wellbeing and calm that I craved, that I used to find halfway down a bottle of red, was about 60 per cent replicated in pizza and pasta and granola with full-cream yoghurt. Man alive, that stuff is good. Even today I have to ration myself with granola. I'd eat the whole box if I could. I can't now, but I could once – and I frequently did. I'd buy a litre of Cape Fruit or strawberry yoghurt, dump half of it into a bowl and pour granola into the carton, and then I'd mix it all up until it formed a sort of edible cement and eat it in front of the television. Sam, meet television; television, meet Sam. I formed a distinctly unhealthy relationship with the TV. It kept me company; it kept me from silence and from being alone with my thoughts. With CNN or a movie channel, I didn't have to think. And *reality* TV! That was the best! I could sit for hours and watch Donald Trump firing people on *The Apprentice*, or flick to BBC Home and watch random interior decorators transforming people's rooms over 24 hours, or to the Series channel to see Jerry Springer exposing yet another cheating scandal, designed and edited so as to shock only the unsuspecting spouse of the adulterer.

It's obvious now that I was groping for numbing substances and circumstances. I knitted a lot as well. I knitted for myself and for other people. I learned to cook without alcohol, although that was another blow. How do you make a port-wine casserole without port? Or a sherry trifle without sherry? Or a port-wine casserole with sherry because you finished the whole bottle of port while chopping onions and browning meat? If you serve enough wine before the meal, no one can taste the difference. I know. I did that.

The first year of sobriety was easy. I say that with hindsight, of course, because at the time it was the hardest year of my life. Perhaps it's more accurate to say it was simpler. All I had to do was not drink. That's all. Look, drinking was everything, so it just felt impossible, but it wasn't impossible. I was aware every waking moment. If you don't think that's possible, then try thinking back to when you were a child the night before your birthday or Christmas. Remember how you were almost sick with excitement? How you couldn't concentrate on anything else? How you lay awake in bed wondering what your presents would be? Well, now take that feeling, flip it over into the negative and that's how I felt every waking minute for a year.

I had a lot of AA literature – I still do. It is all very well thumbed now, although I don't think I've touched it as much in the past 13 years as I did in the first year. It became a little loose-leaf bible, a series of instructions to get me through each day. This one especially:

Just for today I will try to live through this day only, and not tackle all my problems at once. I can do something for twelve hours that would appall me if I felt I had to keep it up for a lifetime.

It couldn't have been truer. I didn't allow myself to think of what the rest of my life would be like without wine. Just that one day. I could do that day. Working on the breakfast show of a major radio station had its pros and cons. The pro was that I got to be creative in an ironclad structure, which was how I would live my life from now on, in ironclad structure. The con was that I finished work midmorning and had the rest of the day to fill on my own. A day on my own was a day full of thoughts, a golden opportunity to dwell on real and imagined wrongs and to torture myself with thoughts of drinking. The antidepressants I had been on for years were now working in the absence of the alcohol that had cancelled them out for a long time. There were side effects; I started feeling removed from life, as though I was seeing everything I used to see, but through a sunroof – all there, but further away.

But my inner circle was strong. Very strong. They nursed me like a sick child. They turned a blind eye to my moods and anxiety and spiky behaviour. They came to visit me when I wouldn't go to them. They ran interference when I wouldn't go somewhere or do something. It was understood that Sam Was Sick and needed tending. And that is what they did.

And that was the first 365 days. Three hundred and sixty-five.

CHAPTER 10

How much is enough?

When I started this chapter I had been sober for five thousand two hundred days. I have now been sober for longer than I was an active alcoholic. In many ways, it gets easier the longer you don't drink. The habit – because that's what it is – is broken. Although there are gaps in the garden of your physical and mental coping mechanisms, the grass grows over them and you begin to function normally again. After a year, I could go out to lunch or dinner and not crave a drink. I could be in a room where other people were drinking and not want to run screaming through a plate-glass door. I'd go home and make tea or coffee or a sandwich instead of lying on the couch clutching a pillow and wondering how long getting to five o'clock would feel.

But other things are more difficult. For everyone else, you are now well. The vigilance with which they watch you has relaxed. That's because you're better now. You must be, or you wouldn't be able to sustain your new way of life; you wouldn't be able to stay dry and aware, which fits in better with their lives anyway. Bit by bit, the constant concern ebbs away until they are getting on with their own lives again.

It's like when someone dies; you drop everything for the bereaved. You call and message every day. You make food so they don't have to and fetch their kids from school and organise snacks for the funeral and stock their fridge. You take care of them until they seem to be able to stand on their own feet again. And then you move on. You call once a week instead of once a day. You offer less. Life continues, and there will be other needs to fulfil, your own included. And that's natural. That's the way of life.

But for those left behind, those trying to rebuild our lives out of the wreckage, it is not over. It is never over. I will never move on; I can only move through it. I've grieved for both deaths, my former self and my mother, so I know.

Over five thousand days later, I am no more complacent about sobriety than I was on the first day, perhaps even less so. Fourteen years is a long time to stay sober. Besides myself and my friend Melinda, who published this book, everyone who got sober at the same time as I did has either relapsed or died, even my original sponsor. She drank herself unconscious eight years into her own sobriety and four years into mine. We had a huge fight about it.

"I think it might have been a phase."

"Don't say that to me – please don't. Not to me."

"I'm older now. I have kids. I'm managing a life."

"Yes! You have kids! So, if you don't have a problem with drinking, then just don't!"

"I helped you when you needed me! So don't judge me now!"

I was totally unmoved.

"I don't judge you. I judge the alcoholic in you and that's the person I'm speaking to. Come back when the sober you takes over."

They were harsh words – and cruel – but I couldn't and wouldn't let myself stand by while she self-destructed. If I okayed her relapse, or – as she was billing it – the start of a new 'phase', I in some way okayed my own. And that was not going to happen. And we didn't speak for another seven years, until she went back to AA.

After a year the cravings were less, but they were no less keen when they did come. But I had a plan. I ate them. I consumed them. I pushed them down and confused the craving for a drink with a craving for burgers and pizza and toasted bacon-egg-and-cheese sandwiches and litre upon litre of Fanta orange. It was a shock to realise that life doesn't magically get better when you get sober. You don't get a key to unlock the secrets of the universe. People don't automatically love you for your immense inner strength. They think – in fact, they're quite sure, and rightly so – that if you had exercised that inner strength a little earlier you might not have become the liability you were for years.

It wasn't a conscious decision to let myself get fat. That was an unfortunate by-product of an otherwise terrific new defence mechanism. The more I ate, the less I wanted to drink. In that first year I put on about seven kilograms. It doesn't sound like that much, seven kilograms. I went from a loose size 36 to a tight 38. I started replacing Medium clothes with Large clothes, but you'd never have looked at me that year and thought, *Wow, she's fat.* A year later you would. Eleven months after I took my last drink I fell pregnant with my first child. The day I found out, I weighed 78 kilograms. The day I gave birth I topped the scale at 102. Kilograms. Two Reese Witherspoons, I reckon. Fat.

CHAPTER 11

A decade on a diet

'Eating moderately' and 'cutting down on drinking' are the same thing. One is embarrassing, shameful and feels kind of futile, and the other is … well, cutting down on drinking: embarrassing, shameful and kind of futile. There are a lot of parallels. The first is denial. As are the second, the third and the fourth. A typical drinking day went like this:

Wake up and rest head on tiles of bathroom wall until throbbing in head stops. Drink water, coffee and ginger ale until lunchtime. Promise to have only two glasses of wine at lunch. Finish bottle, plus one glass of port, plus one more glass of port. Go home and sleep and then start preparing dinner. Promise to have only two glasses of wine for dinner. Finish bottle, plus half bottle of something else from back of cupboard, plus whiskey. Hate self. Go to bed, last waking thought being, *I will start being moderate tomorrow.*

A typical eating day went like this:

Wake up and rest head on bathroom tiles while standing on scale and pretending weight will be the same standing straight up as it is while pressing another part of body against something else. If it's not a good weight, repeat process two more times and take best of three. Drink water and black coffee until lunch. Promise to only eat salad for lunch. Eat salad for lunch. And bread. And cheese and crumbed chicken – and carrot cake because it's not that fattening because it has carrots in it. Have an afternoon sleep and then start preparing dinner. Promise to have steamed vegetables and fish for dinner cooked in a steamer purchased especially. Eat carrot cake while waiting for fish and veggies to steam. Because carrots. Hate self. Go to bed, last waking thought being, *I will start being moderate tomorrow*.

Look, I tried. No one can say I didn't try. I was the Riaan Manser of diets; there were no limits. Can't be done? I'll do it. Not going to work? I'll work it. Could be life-threatening? Bring it on!

I tried everything, and in every permutation. I forgot more than I remembered. I had 37 diet books. Thirty-seven. They filled a whole shelf of the bookcase. Two of them were the same diet. Either I had liked it so much I had tried it twice or I had forgotten I'd already done it. The more extreme the diet the better! Who wanted to weigh out 115 grams of chicken when you could just strike out an entire food group? I peed into cups. I had blood tests. I monitored my menstrual cycle.

But I'm getting ahead of myself here. I didn't do any of this straight away. I didn't do it for a long time.

By the time I gave birth to Christopher I topped the scale at 102 kilograms. The scale had never gone into triple figures before. It should have filled me with horror, but it didn't. I felt curiously proud. I had broken a barrier, moved a goalpost, shifted a boundary. In hindsight, it was exactly the same experience, minus the headache, as I would get after a night of extreme drinking. Waking up surrounded by bottles should be a sobering experience, but I would feel that same warped sense of pride. Twelve green bottles. Twelve litres of vanilla ice cream. I was still alive. And awake. I had survived all the punishment I'd put my body though. I was stronger than I had thought. Inebriation and obesity, sisters under the skin. And, anyway, I was pregnant; the weight would fall off once I had my baby.

But the weight did not fall off once I had my baby. The six kilograms of child, placenta and amniotic fluid were gone, sure, but what was left was 96 kilograms of me. There was an awful lot of me to love. And I didn't love any of it.

I tortured my nearest and dearest with my insecurities.

"I'm *sooo* fat!" I would wail to Martin.

"You're not that fat," he would say, desperately searching for an exit.

"So you agree with me! I'm fat!"

He was trapped and he knew it.

"You're a bit bigger than you used to be, but it's fine – I love you just the way you are."

"But I'm *huge!*"

"You've just had a baby," he'd protest weakly. "Give it time. I'll call you from work."

And he'd run like a dog who's just heard the word 'bath'.

You are only allowed to use the 'just had a baby' excuse after you've just had a baby. I used it for years.

I searched for medical explanations for why I ate so compulsively. Was it normal for a woman to put on 25 kilograms during pregnancy and only lose six after the birth? Well, that's not strictly true. The needle on the scale dropped to 92 kilograms and sat there.

Mirror, mirror, on the wall, who is the fattest of them all?

Look at the scale, love – there's your answer.

There was no medical explanation for why I ate so compulsively. It was habit. A habit that had started during the first year of sobriety and it ratcheted up the ante during pregnancy. I was terribly sick through my first trimester and half of my second, and it took me a while to realise that the extreme nausea was combatted by the act of eating, and not the food itself. To this day, almost 13 years on, I cannot look at a ginger biscuit. In my first trimester I was eating a packet a day. And that wasn't all.

I laugh so hard every time some celebrity comes out with the old "If you're craving it your body needs it" adage, because it's usually the reason someone who generally exists on mosquitos and lettuce gives for turning to cheese and bread. I don't know what need my body thought it was fulfilling by egging me on to give in to my cravings, but I struggle to believe that shocking pink viennas on soft white rolls with tomato sauce and American mustard was fulfilling some nutritional shortcoming. And I ate six of those a day. Yes, really. Six. I would buy a packet of six hotdog rolls on the way home from work and defrost some tubes of what looked like nuclear waste in cerise and consume them throughout the day. And when I had finished those I would turn to ice lollies. Orange ones. They were orange in name and orange in colour. I don't think they had ever seen an actual orange. They didn't even taste citrusy. But they were cold sticks of sugary goodness and I could do four boxes of eight in a week. And I did. The average-sized pregnant woman is supposed to put on between one and two kilograms in the first trimester. I picked up eight. When my baby was born I lost less weight at his birth than I gained in the first three months of being pregnant. How about that? Overachieving again.

I didn't just eat to quell the nausea. I ate to quell the cravings for wine. I'd gone months without any kind of regular need for a drink. The desire was there, sure, and the occasional wistful memory, but the cravings were few and far between. Now they were daily. I would sit on the bathroom floor with my head resting against the toilet seat and wish and wish for a cold glass of wine. A glass of wine would just take the edge off. If I had a rand for every time that phrase 'take the edge off' entered my thoughts, I would have paid off my bond by the end of that trimester. Those thoughts shook me to the core. I felt like a cartoon character, a good angel on one shoulder, a bad angel on the other. And they fought. They fought so hard.

There's a fable about an old man who tells his grandson a tale about the battle that goes on inside all of us. He says, "There are two wolves inside us all. One is evil and angry and envious and sorrowful and guilty and resentful and filled with self-pity. The other is good and joyful and hopeful and kind and honest and faithful and filled with compassion."

The grandson thinks about this for a while and then asks, "Which wolf wins?"

The old man replies, "The one you feed."

I fed the good wolf. I fed it until it was choking while the bad one starved. I anaesthetised it with white bread and pink sausages and orange water lollies. Feeling so desperate for alcohol was both terrifying and comforting. Terrifying because it was so real and so illogical and so strong, and comforting because it was so real and illogical and strong. I knew wanting anything so obviously bad for me and potentially life-threatening for my baby was beyond my control. It wasn't about willpower; it was about accepting that there was a chemical force inside me that I couldn't get rid of, or control. I could only try to manage it.

And I did manage it. I managed it brilliantly. I'm not afraid to say so. It is the thing I have done in my life of which I am most proud. When I look back over my life and my career, three bestselling books and a sell-out play and almost 20 years on breakfast radio, I am most proud of staying sober through both of my pregnancies when every nerve was screaming for drunken oblivion.

It was the hardest thing I have ever done. And I managed. I didn't go back.

I did, however, pick up 25 kilograms.

When I talk about being fat now, it ruffles a lot of feathers. It's as though the use of the word 'fat' is in some way derogatory. It isn't for me. It's the truth. I was fat. I was extremely fat. In fact, when I calculated my Body Mass Index at the time, it was 31.5, which is clinically obese. I didn't think of it like that though. I kept thinking of my overstretched body as a sort of waiting room from whence, when the time was right, the real me would emerge. The thin, sober, energetic me. But I didn't put a time frame on that. None at all. I put my 'thin clothes' away for when I was thin again, I bought a lot of stretch jeans and big floral shirts and comfortable shoes because – and you won't necessarily think of this until you're in the same position – the more you weigh, the more you carry. You feel it in your feet, not to mention your knees.

I, however, moved around – albeit more slowly – in a bubble of benign blindness. I treated my weight much the same way I think the average government ministry seems to treat problems. First, a committee will establish a working group to compile an independent report, which will be edited and audited and then fed back to whomever compiled it in the first place, who promptly deposits it on a 'things to action' pile and immediately does nothing.

It seems incredible now, but at the time I refused to realise how big I had got. On my wedding day five years previously, I had been 65 kilograms. Four years later I had stopped drinking and had a baby and the difference between then and now was 27 kilograms, minus the baby weight. I had put on almost half of my body weight again. And, yes, I know that's possible because, look, I did it! But what I can't explain is how I accepted it for so long. I didn't try to lose weight for ages, not seriously. I carried on eating. And while I ensured that my son was eating sugar-free, organic, free-range everything, I was wolfing down toast and butter, and packets of cereal, with and without milk, and litres and litres of my beloved ice cream. I was the embodiment of the double standard. I didn't want him to end up like me. Of course, it is only much later that you realise as a mother that they do as you do, they don't do as you say.

Being fat was comforting, in the same way being drunk was comforting. A myth I am always eager to dispel is that the bigger you are, the more noticeable. It's actually the other way around, the bigger you are the more you fade into the background, the less attention you attract. It's not spotlight stuff, the way falling off a table at New Year's is, although you don't feel that either really if you're drunk because (a) your pain receptors are on a work-to-rule, and (b) you can tell yourself that if you don't remember it, it never happened.

I could push Chris up and down the road in his pram in the sunshine and listen to him gurgling happily and feel very peaceful. It didn't matter how big I was. The more fat I carried, the more insulated I felt from the pressures and stresses of life outside. And fat is a form of insulation in more ways than one. You can go unnoticed. I wasn't anxious or panicky for most of the time I was really big. Every time I worried about something or felt insecure, I just ate something. Easy. Some people drink to feel something; I drank to feel nothing. And that's why I ate as well.

The bigger I got the smaller my world became. I didn't

out much, except to work and the shops and the odd breakfast with friends. On the show, I was the perfect mix of *Yes, Dear* and acerbic wit, and yet at home the wittiest thing I did was play peekaboo with Christopher. My most intellectual conversations were with my son and singing along to *Balamory* and *Barney* isn't really a universally recognised form of sparkling wit and personality. And I didn't mind. It was safe. I lived the cliché of the overweight mommy, eating toddler leftovers like the vacuum cleaner on *Teletubbies*. As Chris progressed to solids, I cooked a lot of comfort food. Kids are supposed to experiment, so I made lasagna and macaroni cheese and cottage pie and chicken strips and fish fingers and broccoli and cauliflower with cheese sauce, and he tried it all and rejected a lot of it and what he didn't eat I finished. If naan bread came with a thread count I would have wrapped myself in it and slept.

Obviously, living life as a human duvet has its drawbacks. I think some people were mildly surprised by how little I had done to get back into shape, particularly as Chris was now walking. A colleague asked if I was worried I might stay that weight forever. My mother would sometimes ask – quite casually, of course – how I was and if I'd managed to get to the gym. I bought a pedometer, a step counter, and I wore it like some lucky amulet to ward off evil. "Look," it said, "she's got this under control! She's counting steps, for God's sake. She's working on it. Leave her alone." I also knew how to head off any weight-related topics. I was always the first person to make the fat joke. Once that was out of the way, everyone could relax. Hell, if I knew I was fat, then it must mean I was okay with it so no one needed to say anything or avoid saying anything. We could all just get on with … well, lunch.

I don't know, even now, whether I realised I had cross addicted. I'd leapfrogged from the lily pad with a wet bar to the lily pad with the 24-hour fast-food joint. You'd think that after years of using the same excuses and lies to myself and others about my drinking, I would have seen this and been able to check myself before doing the same thing with eating.

The diet starts tomorrow.

Okay, well just one more.

No, I honestly can't. I promised myself I wouldn't.

I think I'm just retaining water.

Yeah, it's always hard to lose those last five (or 27) kilos.

I may as well just finish this cake, 'cos then there will be nothing to tempt me tomorrow.

There're actually more calories in a granola bar than a KitKat.

Yeah. No.

Denial, denial, denial.

I honestly didn't see in the mirror what I see now when I look at pictures from back then. But I think I must have known subconsciously that I wasn't the prettiest cup in the tea set. There aren't many photographs of me at my largest, and in those that do exist I generally have a child on my lap or am standing behind something.

And when I started buying all my clothes from the 'leisurewear' sections at Woolworths, which is basically baggy T-shirts and tracksuits, I must have known. How could I not? Did I really not see that by buying four tracksuits and alternating tops and bottoms as my daily wardrobe was flying the proverbial white flag from the top of cellulite hill?

Perhaps I didn't let myself think about it too hard because at that time I was buying huge slabs of chocolate on the way home from work and telling myself it was cheaper than buying smaller bars and that I would make them last for two days. I never did. I did the same with ice cream. I'd buy two litres because it was more economical and would take longer to finish. It didn't. I'd make an enormous dish of macaroni cheese so we could eat it for dinner two nights in a row. Then I'd sneak into the kitchen in the dead of night and grate more cheese over the top and finish it. I was hungry, I would tell myself. But I wasn't really. It wasn't about what I was eating, it was about what was eating me.

While all this was happening, my body was giving me trouble on a different level. My back hurt all the time. I had a car accident four and a half months into carrying Chris and hurt my back and it had never really recovered. For the last 10 weeks of my pregnancy I was in pain all the time, but I attributed that to a big baby positioned awkwardly and kept telling myself that once I'd given birth and lost all the baby weight (yes, that again), everything would return to normal. Well, it didn't – and not just because I was still a body double for the Michelin Man. I had osteoarthritis. Every morning I woke up in pain and every night I went to bed the same way. Being overweight did not help; in fact, being overweight was a major contributing factor. It was a vicious circle: I ate to feel better and made myself feel worse. Rinse and repeat. But in that washing cycle I didn't come out fresh and sparkly clean; I flopped out the washing machine like an ageing dishcloth. The eating I was doing to deaden the pain was doing just the opposite.

You'd think, in the face of such overwhelming evidence that my weight had gone beyond being aesthetically displeasing and entered the realm of physically debilitating, the most obvious course of action would be to make a concerted effort to lose some of it. And you'd be right. Just as, if you'd been standing next to me that morning I looked at myself in the bathroom mirror six months before my last glass of wine, you'd have seen it was time to stop drinking. But eating less and exercising more still weren't on my list of things to do. I was too busy on the internet, researching every other conceivable reason I might be fat. If I could find another cause I might not have to change my behaviour patterns, patterns that were so destructively comforting.

"I think I am insulin resistant!" I announced proudly to my husband over dinner.

He eyed me cautiously over his glasses. He had long ago adopted the Swiss approach. Neutrality at all costs.

"Okay ..."

"Yes. It would explain everything."

"Okay," he said gingerly.

"Yes, it's if you have high insulin levels and then you get resistant to it and then you put on weight. I think it's kind of like that."

Martin did not look convinced. But I persisted.

"And if you are insulin resistant you can just take stuff and then it regulates it and then you lose weight," I said brightly.

He got up from the table.

"I have a conference call," he said with barely disguised relief.

"But it's seven o clock!"

"Yes, it's with America."

I think Martin was grateful many times that he worked for an international company.

"So I'm going to go for blood tests to see," I called after him.

"You do that," he replied.

I was not insulin resistant.

Undaunted, I also had my thyroid checked, my iron levels and my hormones. The vein in my left arm got a proper seeing to.

I did not have an over- or under-active thyroid, my iron levels were just fine and my hormone levels were A-Okay. I was also *not* allergic to gluten or casein, and I was not lactose intolerant. I was just fat.

I made the odd half-hearted attempt to eat less. I knew I had to do something about my weight; I was in pain almost all the time. But a diet? What if eating less made me want to drink again? Wasn't it better to be fat and aware than drunk and impaired? That question hovered in the forefront of my mind all the time. But I didn't see an alternative. If I was going to be able to get from the bed to the bathroom first thing in the morning without limping I was going to have to give eating less a go. But, wait, maybe there was one more option …

I had a friend whose mother was a retired doctor who could still write prescriptions and she said she could help me. And, much as I like doing everything on my own, I was tired of sleeping with a pillow between my legs and a hot pack draped over my hip, so I went to see her.

"Now, how can I help you?" She was warm and calm and had a lovely bedside manner. I knew I would be okay.

"Well …"

I told her all about it. About the car accident and birth and postnatal depression and feeling like a wendy house in velour pants. And she listened and made notes and nodded and I relaxed.

"I can help you," she said, reaching for her prescription pad. "I'm going to prescribe you a painkiller ..."

And you know if she had stopped there, or even after the muscle relaxant or even after the other thing I'd have to take if I took those two things to combat the nausea that would result in combining the first two, I might have gone along with it. But as the list got longer and she tore off the top page and started writing on the other side, I started to feel uneasy.

"Here you go," she said.

"See how the first month goes and if it's helping I'll give you a six-month repeat."

I thanked her and left and went to sit in my car with that piece of paper in my hand. And then I looked at myself in the rear-view mirror.

"You're a fat alcoholic," said the Sam in the mirror.

"I'm a fat alcoholic who is in pain."

The me in the mirror was not at all sympathetic.

"If you take all those pills, you will have a whole new problem to deal with. And you might not be able to come back from this one."

"But I'm sore. I'm sore all the time," I wanted to cry. I was so disappointed and frustrated. I had a solution in my hand, but I knew it was no solution at all.

Mirror Sam was relentless.

"Then lose some fucking weight, bitch."

Mirror Sam was right.

"Lose some fucking weight because we are not going back to where we were two years ago. We. Are. Not."

I looked at the piece of paper. It would be so easy.

Then I tore it in half.

"Okay, then."

And I went home and threw it away. And the next day I joined Weightwatchers. Cos I'm gangsta like that.

Weightwatchers was my first proper, real, official attempt to lose weight. And it really is official, I must tell you. First you find a group near you. Then you join up. The group leader weighs you, and then you calculate your goal weight – or rather, they calculate your goal weight. And then you get a whole lot of literature and a book of points.

The points book is your food bible. Each and every food under the sun has an allocation of points. I marvelled at this. How did they work this out? There are so many foods! And so many permutations of these foods! Take milk, for example: they had points for full cream and skimmed and semi skimmed and low fat and fat free and *all* of those were different! And milk was an easy one – you should have seen the bread section. A full page devoted to bread! There was white bread and brown bread and wholegrain bread and rye bread and low-GI bread and berlinerbrot, which is apparently a type of rye but not exactly the same as the other rye, and there was high-fibre bread and bread rolls, white and brown and big and small. I was terribly impressed. I took everything home and studied the book for ages. I was allowed 24 points a day, which is quite a lot if you learn all the foods and eat a lot of low-fat stuff. There were only two drawbacks to Weightwatchers. One was that you could use all your points for a day if you ate three slices of pizza, and the other was the weigh-in.

The weigh-in was the dread of my week. This was the reminder that someone besides you really was watching your weight. I would arrive every Wednesday at 1 pm at the Sandton library, which is where my group would meet, and all of us members would dutifully stand in line waiting for the news of whether or not we had succeeded in our weight-loss goal for the week. You cannot fudge the issue at Weightwatchers. (Well, at Weightwatchers there shouldn't be any fudge at all really.) Not only is it a public weigh-in, but they record your results in your little book and you get a stamp. A stamp. Like the ones you got in school if your handwriting was especially neat or if the teacher had run out of gold stars. And if you missed a weigh-in it would show because you wouldn't have a dated stamp. It would show that you had *bunked*. Our group leader was very strict. She was like a gym teacher, very cheerful and full of life and absolutely terrifying. I once played a whole hockey match at school with a sprained ankle because I was too afraid to tell the sports mistress.

Some people looked forward to the weigh-in. The rest of us hated those people. They were the type of people who, at school, would put their hands up to clean the blackboard or ask for more paper during an exam.

"I've been *so* good this week," they would say excitedly.

Did you help an old lady across a road or give money to an animal shelter? I would want to ask. Because that's what being *so* good should be about. But when you're fat, overweight or just 'carrying a few extra kilograms', your definitions of such terms as 'good' and 'bad' narrow to how closely or how loosely you have stuck to your points that week. Being 'good' means you didn't look right or left in the checkout aisle full of chocolates at Woolworths. Being 'bad' meant you'd eaten enough pizza to use up the points of three people.

There were some tricks to the weigh-in. If I was going to cheat during the week – and I was, I knew I was – I would do it on weigh-in day *after* the weigh in. Then I knew I would have a full six days to 'lose the evidence' and more until the next opportunity for public humiliation.

I hasten to say, though, that there was no deliberate attempt made to humiliate us. No one shouted out, "Ha, you're up! You great big pork pie!" But as one person stepped on the scale and either fist-pumped the air or withered like a dry leaf in a flame, we all knew and the news would make its way down the line.

"Shame, she's put on 200 grams."

"Ah no, man! And she was doing so well ..."

"Yeah, she says she doesn't know what happened."

We would all nod sadly. There was nothing worse than not knowing what happened.

Another trick was to eat and drink nothing that day. From sun-up, I would behave as though I was about to have an operation under general anaesthetic: nil by mouth from 10 pm the night before. Also, no gym in the morning, or any form of strenuous activity, in case I 'retained water'. You could pick up a fair bit on the scale from water retention. I know because it was your ace in the hole if you had overindulged that week. Especially if you were a woman.

"Sam, you're up a bit."

"I know, Nicky," I'd whisper – she was my group leader – eyes darting around to see whether anyone was listening. "But I'm expecting my period."

"Ah," she'd nod understandingly. "That makes sense. So it will be better next week."

I'd agree enthusiastically, go and have my weekly ice cream and eat like a Spartan for the next week to make that statement a reality.

You had to make a note of when you used that excuse though, because it was only taken as valid one week in four. And, of course, only for girls.

The other place you could buy yourself some wiggle room was with your shoes. For reasons of hygiene, I think (I never asked), you had to weigh in wearing your shoes. If you forgot and wore boots you were lost. A pair of boots would send your measurement skyrocketing and Nicky didn't give you any leeway on shoes. She said, quite rightly, that you should weigh in the same clothes and shoes each week and, funnily enough, a lot of us did. Anyone seeing us on a weekly basis would have thought we all had our own individual uniforms. A very clever girl used to keep in her bag those silly little slippers they give you for free at a spa when you go for a massage and if she had eaten past her points limit during the week, she would slip off her real shoes and weigh in in those. Nicky would frown but she would let it slide. And of course in winter you'd weigh more in a sweater so we would all stand there in our shirt sleeves shivering with cold.

A week could be made or broken on that weigh-in. I used to sit next to a very charming gay couple during meetings. I think that was the other reason I tried Weightwatchers first – because of the meetings. I was an old hat at those. I'd had a few years of sitting with like-minded souls, bonded together in a common understanding of our own weakness. I slid into that unspoken camaraderie with ease. It doesn't matter who you are or where you come from, if you're drunk or high or fat, there's a group. Go to it.

The couple lived together. They gymmed together. It was a match made in heaven. They readily agreed that moving in together had made them just a little too comfortable around the buffet table, but they would lose the weight and it would be yet another thing they would do together. And it was all going swimmingly until the day one of them dropped a kilogram more than the other.

"I don't understand," said the other, his voice tremulous.

"We've eaten everything the same; we do the same routine at gym ... What's happened?"

"Cheer up," said the champion, trying to be helpful. "Maybe next week you'll catch up!"

The rest of us winced.

The first leapt up and grabbed his wallet and keys.

"You always have to be the overachiever in this relationship!"

He burst into tears and ran out, his partner following anxiously behind.

Awkward.

I wish Weightwatchers had worked for me. Or that I had worked for Weightwatchers. But it wasn't them; it was me. I got obsessed with the points system to the point of neurosis. One evening, my friend Alex finally snapped.

"Put it away," she hissed through gritted teeth.

My points book was open on the table in the restaurant.

"I will in a minute. Just need to work out what I can have."

I had eaten nothing that day because I knew I was going out to dinner. This meant I had taken all my medication on an empty stomach. This is never a good idea.

"You can have anything you want within reason," she said in that voice she used when she was trying to be calm when she was feeling anything but.

"No I can't. I can have anything I want *within my points*. Give me a minute. And a pen."

I was trying to work out what combination of food I could eat that would constitute a meal that would fill me up without blowing my points allocation.

Without a word, she passed me a pen.

"Okay, so if I have pasta arrabbiata and I only have half a bowl with Parmesan cheese ... or two thirds of a bowl without cheese, and a Diet Coke, then that works out to ..." I was adding and subtracting like a ten-year-old with a story sum: "Sam has 24 points. If a cup of pasta is five points and Sam has three cups plus half a cup of arrabbiata sauce plus two teaspoons of Parmesan cheese ..."

Sam gave up. I put the book back in my bag.

"I'll worry about it tomorrow," I said. And ordered pasta and loaded it with many teaspoons of Parmesan cheese. And I had dessert. I had cheesecake. Which was about ten million points.

Alex shook her head.

"You can't live like this, Sam. You can't seriously police everything you eat."

But I'd done it before. And I was my own law and order. And it had worked; it was working with drink. Why couldn't I make it work with food? Probably because I was still looking for the loopholes, the same loopholes that had sent my 'two weeks of no drinking' mission crashing and burning 10 days into it, the same loopholes that made me buy bigger and bigger wine glasses until I was practically drinking out of a vase, just so I could keep telling myself I was only drinking two glasses of wine at a time. The other reason I was struggling was because when you stop drinking you stop. Full stop. No more. Never. Ever. You can't stop eating. You have to eat to live. I just needed to find a way to stop living to eat.

That wasn't the final straw for my relationship with Weight-watchers, by the way. The final straw was when Nicky caught me in Milky Lane ordering a strawberry sundae. As she looked at me open-mouthed through the window, I felt like a husband who's been caught with his hand up his secretary's skirt. I briefly considering shouting, "It's not what it looks like!" but I didn't. It was exactly what it looked like. I was too embarrassed to go back to the group after that. I decided whatever I did next, I would do it alone.

What I decided to do next was have a blood test. I found a book called *Eat Right for Your Type* by Peter J D'Adamo. If you ate according to your blood group, you couldn't help but lose weight and live a better and healthier life. I didn't care about living a better or healthier life. I wanted a thinner life. I bought the book and went for a blood test. I made Martin come with me and have a blood test. I was A-negative. He was O-positive. That was our first problem.

Type A is mainly vegetarian, with light exercise and meditation. It seemed a sort of cheesecloth-and-sandals approach to life. Type O was no grains, loads of meat and vigorous exercise.

"Are we going to cook two meals a night?" asked Martin suspiciously.

"No, we'll cook meat and vegetables and quinoa and you'll eat the meat and vegetables and I'll eat the vegetables and quinoa."

It lasted four weeks. I've never been so grumpy for such a concentrated period of time. I hated buckwheat and sprouted wheat and kasha. I didn't like tamari – it was like soy sauce with no balls. There was no sugar (although what diet has?); I was bloated and irritable, and it didn't help that my husband was in seventh heaven. He had been a meat-and-potatoes man his whole life and now he had a medical stamp of approval to indulge. It also didn't help that he lost two kilograms and I hadn't lost a gram.

"I'm not doing this any more," I announced at dinner.

He paused over his steak.

"I'm enjoying it, and I've lost weight."

"Well, I'm not and I'm still fat."

"Okay?"

"So you can carry on, but I'm going to do something else, or I'll just be irritable all the time."

Cue conference call with America. Exit Martin stage left.

I was undaunted. With every diet came a new way to make good. There were pages to be turned, fat to be lost, jeans to fit into. I still had a pair of Levi's from before I fell pregnant with Chris. I'd been sober for about 10 months and I'd picked up seven kilos already. So what does a girl do when she's depressed about her weight? She goes shopping! Although maybe she shouldn't go shopping for jeans ...

I was browsing the different shapes in the Levi Store when one of the assistants slid up to me.

"Can I help you?'

"Yes please!" I said. "I'd like these in a size 32."

He smirked.

"You sure you want a 32?"

I was sure. I said so.

"Should I give you a 34 as well, just to, like, *try?*"

"No, that's okay, thanks. I'll just take a 32."

I was smarting when I got to the changing room. Just who did he think he was?

He thought he was someone who was right about my new size. And he was. I couldn't get the 32 past my thighs. I sat on the floor and wondered what to do. Would a different style fit differently? I didn't think so. Damn.

"So, can I get you a 34?" he asked smugly, as I joined him at the till, jeans slung over one arm.

"No thank you – these fit perfectly," I said.

And I bought them.

They would fit perfectly one day, I was sure. Well, nearly sure. Well ... hopeful.

I bought lots of books. Lots and lots and lots. I bought *The Hip Chick's Guide to Macrobiotics*. That was a short-lived and painful exercise. The way I chose my diets was to find pictures of skinny people and then research them to see what diets they were on. You could discount most of the supermodels instantly; half of them didn't eat anything and the other half said they ate whatever they wanted. Lies and deceit!

The Series channel was running a lot of old eighties' series and I blame that for most of my retro diets. Dirk Benedict from *The A-Team* was a follower of the macrobiotic diet and he looked amazing! Suzanne Somers, from *Three's Company*, was another one. She advocated (still does) some food combining and ways to eat different stuff and it all seemed suspiciously easy. There was no way anything that easy could work, I was certain. If I wasn't suffering, I wasn't dieting, right? I took the excess of my drinking days and turned it into deprivation. George Ohsawa, one of the people credited with opening up macrobiotics to the West said, "Whatever has a front has a back and the bigger the front, the bigger the back." Yin and Yang. And I lived it; not consciously, but I did. Maximum suffering would equal maximum results. Macrobiotics was the best example of that. It involved a complete clean-out of every cupboard. You eat a lot of grains. And a lot of beans. A *lot* of beans. It is a very antisocial diet. And I dragged poor Martin on this diet journey as well.

"When can we have meat again?" he asked plaintively, picking at his pickled cabbage and amaranth.

"Well, we can have fish occasionally," I said.

"I don't want fish occasionally; I want a steak now."

I couldn't blame him. The grain thing got me down. There should have been a supplementary pamphlet called *Making Brown Rice Fun*.

Martin pushed his plate back.

"I think I'll just have a cheese sandwich."

Pause.

"Uhm, there isn't any bread. Or cheese."

He stared at me stonily.

"Why not?"

"Because dairy isn't good for us. Neither is bread."

Silence.

"But I'm planning to make some sprouted grain bread tomorrow," I said cheerily.

Martin had had enough. This poor patient man finally cracked.

"That's enough, Sam," he hissed through clenched jaws. "I'm not doing this any more; it's horrible. I feel like I'm being punished every night! I drive home dreading dinner. I don't know what awful thing you will have cooked up!"

I was hurt, but he was right.

So my diet journey continued alone. As it should probably have started.

For the next two years I explored many options. I tried one diet in which you drink two nutritional (read: tastes of sand) shakes per day and eat one healthy meal. I am of the opinion that I could have drunk two full-fat ice-cream-based milkshakes loaded with cream and bits of chocolate biscuit and one healthy meal and I would still have lost weight, but of course I didn't. My mind couldn't get itself around two milkshakes and a plate of fish as my limit for the day.

Then I tried something that involved me eating broccoli and mozzarella sticks twice a day and with an occasional apple and some crispbread thrown in. I became a disciple of Nicki Waterman, a British fitness expert who wrote books on sugar addiction. I still ate sugar, but I was comforted by the presence of a book that would help me stop eating sugar in case I ever wanted to. If I had lost a kilogram for every book I bought I'd have been well within my healthy BMI range very quickly. I went in at the problem from every angle.

I went the psychological route with Dr Phil McGraw's *The Ultimate Weight Solution*. I felt terrible pressure when I bought that. The use of the word 'ultimate' seems terribly final, as though if I fail the ultimate solution then I have exhausted all avenues of hope. I actually scared myself into losing a few kilograms with Dr Phil. I went the holistic route when I followed Patrick Holford for a while. *Optimum Nutrition made Easy*. Then I read all sorts of articles about him, questioning his credentials – apparently he's not a real doctor – and promptly 'unfollowed' him. That was a bit of a relief actually. I was taking so much vitamin C at that point that my urine was yellow. It was like lemon cordial in the toilet bowl every morning. Weird and disconcerting.

Then there was Gillian McKeith. I blame BBC Prime for that one. She was the presenter of a show called *You Are What You Eat*. The premise was that she was 'invited' into the homes of obese people, some morbidly so, to show them – in as humiliating a fashion as possible – the error of their gluttonous ways. Some of her methods included showing them a table weighed down with a week's worth of their diet, where often the only green stuff on display was jelly babies, examining their stool in front of them and then making them go through colonic irrigation on screen. She was hideous. I devoured every programme as though it was choc-mint ice cream.

That diet was the most expensive I ever followed, but it did work for the two months I tried it. Just be sure and understand that you can never go out to eat again and will have to take out a second bond if you wish to consume blue-green algae as often as she would like. Also, the second you eat dairy, it's over. For a yoghurt fiend like me it was never going to end well.

I went to see a dietician, chiefly because somebody who was a friend of somebody who worked with somebody's brother who was a colleague of a friend had been to see the same woman and said she was amazing. With her, you could eat all your favourite foods. I doubted that. She didn't know my favourite foods were all out of a carton, a packet or a cardboard box. I was right. She tried though, bless her.

"So, if you eat carefully, you can definitely eat chocolate!"

"Really?" I was dubious. I was clutching a sheaf of papers peppered with dirty phrases like 'tuna in spring water' and 'whole grain' and 'fat free'. Fat free is fun free, so let's just call it that. They were not my favourite foods. They were the foods that she told me would be my favourite foods.

"Really." She was so sure. "And if you want chocolate you can have some every day."

That didn't seem right. I probed further.

"Every day? Every single day?"

She nodded vigorously.

"Yes. Two squares of dark chocolate every night."

And there was the catch. I couldn't possibly eat two squares of dark chocolate a night. A bar of chocolate is at least eight squares. There was no chance I could put six squares back in the fridge. It wasn't about willpower. It was beyond the realm of possibility. I told her so.

"Why don't you just try?"

It sounded so easy. And so horribly familiar. Just try. Just try not to drink too much. Well, yes, I could try. I could also try walking on burning coals – and I would probably be more successful. I wanted to weep when I heard that. *Just try*. I *had* tried. God, I had tried and tried and tried. I couldn't. There were no dimmer switches on my different appetites. There was on and off. That's it.

I tried to find a loophole. Does that sound familiar?

"What if I only ate chocolate every four days, but ate the whole slab?"

She shook her head.

"That won't work. It's learning moderation. You want to break that habit."

Well, yes, I want to. And with drinking I could. Eating is more than habit though.

I bought hardcore books, like *Skinny Bitch* and *Run Fat B!tch Run* and *Fat Ass No More!* I didn't like those. I wallowed in enough self-loathing already – I didn't need to be sworn at as well. Those were purchased during my more depressed periods. In retrospect, they were never going to work. If waking up hungover with unexplained bruises and an angry husband wasn't enough to shame me into quitting alcohol, how did I think being called a fat ass bitch was going to make me lose weight?

I bought gentle books like *The Four-Day Win* by the lovely Martha Beck, who caringly suggested that if you can do something for four days you can stick with it. I read that while munching on a carton of Pringles and I agreed. If I could put the Pringles away for four days, I was sure I could put them away for even longer. It was putting them down in the first place that was the trick.

And all the time, there was relapse after relapse. I sat in that river in Egypt and did maths and accounting on how much food I could have and when. I've been thin for a while now and all the things they say about thin people are true. Healthily thin people eat what they want and when they want, because they instinctively make the right choices. And they eat when they are hungry and they stop when they are full. Unless they are thin because they live on nervous energy, coffee and cigarettes, or they forget to eat because they are busy or stressed, that is how people keep the weight off. Most of the time I do that. And most of the time I am eating in the open as opposed to looking for loopholes. The accounting that went into my weightier days was heroically comprehensive. If I have a Diet Coke, I can have a slice of cake. If I have fruit salad with low-fat yoghurt, I can have granola with it. If I eat a muffin, but skip breakfast ... If I eat from the buffet, but don't have dinner ...

I sat solo on a seesaw, perched precariously in the middle, veering wildly from side to side, trying to keep a balance between moderation and excess and failing. Taking your average is not living in moderation. It's the same as drinking hard for four days of the week, taking three days off, and saying, "Well, I only drink a certain amount a day." That's not the middle road – it's running between train tracks trying not to get hit by the trains going in opposite directions and frequently getting splattered across the front of one of them.

CHAPTER 12

The seesaw

I did lose weight. It took two years and many diets and shakes and eating at specific times of the day and food combining. I changed my eating patterns regularly. I also got bored very quickly.

Nothing I did was sustainable in the long term – at least not for me – but in bits and pieces, 500 grams here and 300 grams there, I dropped 20 of the 25 kilograms I had picked up. I was no longer obese; I was chubby. Or curvy, depending on who you talked to. I choose chubby. The one thing that has kept me sober for as long as I have been is that since becoming sober I have never lied to myself about my drinking. Sure, you can lie to others, but never to yourself. It's that level of falsehood that keeps you in denial. I have to keep myself firmly on the side of honesty; it's futile sitting on the fence between heavy drinker and alcoholic, and overweight and curvy. Futile and painful. You get a sore arse.

"It's a good thing you lost the weight slowly; that way it will stay off." Read any health magazine or blog and it will tell you that. Lose weight slowly and steadily on a balanced diet. My life on a diet was anything but balanced. It was the toddler of diets, trying to stay upright, lurching from chair to table leg to doorjamb. It would pause to catch its breath and then it would take another breath and push forward again. And I was almost at my destination when I got pregnant again. My heart was ecstatic. My jeans said … *Rats!*

Depending on how you look at it, I was lucky that, despite having a job in front of the camera, my weight wasn't a problem. *Great Expectations* was a show about twentieth-century parenting and I was a twentieth-century parent. And I actually was, although I hadn't planned it that way. I was pregnant for the first season of the show and having a pregnant host was a bit of a plus. As my waistline grew, so did the audience. I went through all the same things they did, and in real time too. It was a relatable show. I wasn't one of those lucky ladies who just carry a small bump in front of them. I was the bump with a head and little arms and legs. And after I had Genevieve I was a slightly smaller bump with more proportionate head and arms and legs.

And people responded; they really did. There was one episode where we had three TV celebrities on the couch, talking about how they maintained their looks and 'got their bodies back' after having a baby. Eat right, get plenty of rest and drink litres and litres of water seemed to be the main pointers. Then a viewer phoned in.

"I used to be like you ladies," she said, her voice cracking with emotion. "I was the kind of person who got up and blow dried my hair every morning and went to gym every evening."

Everyone nodded understandingly. I nodded too – except about the gym part. I had only ever made a cameo appearance at gym. If gym was a movie I'd be the extra, stage left, puzzling over the Smith machine.

"And now my baby is five weeks old and I'm still not back in a routine," she wept. "I haven't washed my hair in days, I wear the same clothes all the time, my jeans don't fit."

Bloody jeans.

"What's wrong with me?"

My heart bled for her.

"You've just had a baby," I said. "That's a Very Big Deal. That's why God invented tracksuits – for postnatal comfort – I'm sure of it."

She giggled a bit. Then Ms Perfect weighed in.

"Just start by putting on a bit of lipstick every day," she said comfortingly. "It makes you feel so much better about yourself."

The giggling stopped.

I was filled with hatred. When I had my first baby the only thing that made me feel so much better about myself was tossing back copious amounts of antidepressants. Oh, and eating bacon sandwiches. For the first six weeks I couldn't have spelled lipstick.

"I wouldn't worry about that," I said, with terrifying niceness. "Just make sure you're getting enough to eat and ask your husband to take the evening feed and then you'll be getting at least one six-hour stint of sleep."

She was crying again.

"You look so nice, Sam," she said. "And you had your baby three months ago."

"Well, yes, I look amazing," I said impatiently, "but I didn't get this way by myself. Two people worked on me for over an hour before I looked like this!"

I gestured to the other ladies on the couch.

"We were all in make-up for ages!"

She was giggling again. I was in full swing now.

"If I had the budget I'd get those two ladies round to my house every morning before work so I could look like this every day! But until then, stretchy jeans, big shirts and occasional lip gloss."

"Okay, Sam," she sniffed.

"Do you feel better?" I was a little worried.

"I do feel better."

I felt less worried.

But that wasn't the end of it.

During the ad break, Ms Perfect tapped me on the knee and shook her head reprovingly.

"You mustn't do that, Sam."

I was confused.

"Do what?"

"Destroy the myth."

More confused.

"But it is a myth. We don't look like this in real life. And we're making that lady feel crap."

"But this is our job, Sam. It inspires confidence that it's possible."

"Yeah, well, I don't think it does."

And certainly for me it was not. I'd put on 25 kilograms with Chris. That's more than two toddlers. I lost 20 and then fell pregnant with Gen and I only put on 11 kilograms. Well, 11.6 … Let's keep the honesty going here. And guess what? I lost 10 of it! So now I was only carrying the five from Chris and the 1.6 from Gen. Oh, and the seven from my first year of sobriety. A mere 13.6. And that was staying put. And, anyway, no one really noticed it. People were used to my earth mother appearance. It was comforting. And it's not like I didn't make an effort. I even eventually joined a gym! I joined a very upmarket, luxurious gym! I joined it before it was finished. It was like buying an apartment off plan. They even had an American sales consultant. Always a slave to clever packaging, I was blown away.

My consultant promised there would be fresh towels, that I wouldn't have to bring my own, so there would be no more soggy gym bag woes when I got home. Someone would press my shirt while I worked out, if I wanted to put on a shirt after I worked out. There would be a jogging track that wrapped around the outside of the building – it'd be like running in the sky! The swimming pool would have soothing lights that changed colour while I swam as gentle music was piped through the water. Oh, and there would be gym equipment. He made that sound almost incidental. Front and centre was the promise that a visit wouldn't just be a workout; it would be an experience. I was sold. I signed up on the spot. I was ready to have several experiences a week! Well, once it opened of course.

When it opened it wasn't exactly as the consultant had promised. The jogging track, which was supposed to be 250 metres long was, for some reason no one could ever explain, only 223. It was very off-putting. On a 250-metre jogging track, you can work out pretty easily that four laps is a kilometre. Eight laps is two kilometres, et cetera, et cetera. On a 223-metre track you had to keep track of your laps and calculate your distance later. Four times around the track was 892 metres. You'd sound like a complete idiot telling people you ran 892 metres. Try it and see.

The pool also provided a slightly different experience to that promised by the consultant. Not only did it not have gentle colour-therapy lights, but the music was non-existent. Or at least I wished it was. There was something wrong with one of the speakers so sometimes, when you swam too near the end of the pool, you'd hear a strange and eerie sound like someone trying to talk to you through a ball of wool. Look, it did make me swim faster on the odd occasion I actually swam, but it wasn't the gentle soothing experience I'd signed up for. In fact, it was a bit like Tindr, a profile picture that promised the world and delivered Alberton. If I could have gone back in time I would have swiped left.

Nevertheless I went three or four times a week for my experience. Sometimes I shuffled along the jogging track, and sometimes I strolled on the treadmill watching music videos on MTV back in the day when they still played music videos on MTV, and watched people using the gym equipment and wondered how they all just knew what it all did. I didn't do much at gym – it was rare that I even broke a sweat – *but* I was going. And my clothes still fit, which was good, and I was still sober, which was better, and I lived in blissful denial about the fact that I was still overweight because no one ever said anything.

Except Roy.

Roy was a boom operator at e.tv and he worked on the *Great Expectations* set. And Roy did not have a filter.

"Sam, do you go to gym?" he asked once.

"Yes, I go four times a week," I said with casual pride.

"You should go more often," he announced to the world at large.

I was shocked.

"Why d'you say that?" I demanded.

"Because you are not pregnant any more, but you still look pregnant," he said, waving his boom mic like a giant fluffy caterpillar on a stick.

I went to the producer, Sally, after the show.

"Am I fat?" I demanded.

(I must pause here to emphasise that I knew I was overweight.

I was in no way in denial about that. I just hadn't let myself think too hard about what other people might be thinking. I think I had fooled myself into thinking that if nobody said anything, then nobody noticed.)

She looked at me blankly.

"What do you mean?"

That's a bad sign. When you are not fat, people answer that question with a quick and emphatic no. They don't play for time by asking you to break down the question for them.

"What do you think I mean? Am I fat?"

She looked at me over the top of her glasses.

"Sam, I don't think anyone would use the word *fat*."

Even worse.

"What word would you use?"

Now she was flapping.

"I don't know! I've never thought about it!"

She paused.

"Your clothes still fit, don't they?"

Well, now that she mentioned it, some of the show wardrobe was a little snug. But only a little. I hadn't been on a scale for a long time. I had a gym membership now – I didn't need a scale. Or did I?

For a long time between pregnancies I had maintained an extremely unhealthy relationship with the bathroom scale. I should really say 'scales' because there had been several. I started with a good old-fashioned spring scale with a pointer, where you stand on it and a little needle springs to the number that corresponds to your weight. That one was my first enemy, and that was backed up by another overweight friend from good old Weightwatchers.

"You can't trust those," she said in the same tone one would use to refer to a 419 scammer. "You have to take a best of three on those."

I already took a best of three on mine. And weighed naked. And rocked forward and backward and to either side like a human skittle, trying to work out a way to get the best result for visible weight loss.

"Scale, scale on the floor, tell me if I've lost some more."

Generally speaking I hadn't.

"You need to get a digital scale," she said. "They also give you your weight down to the nearest decimal point."

And when you're trying to lose weight, every gram counts. A day can be made or broken by a scale reading of 81.4 as compared to 81.2.

So I consigned my vintage scale to the bathroom cupboard to be used as a luggage scale when we travelled, and went out and bought a digital scale.

I hated the digital scale.

The digital scale had me weighing in at a full 600 grams more than the prehistoric scale.

But never mind – I was up for the challenge.

Eventually.

But, for the time being, I had put it in the bathroom cupboard with its vintage mate.

Now, after Roy, I hauled it out again. Was Roy right? Was Sally's avoidance of my question real or imagined?

Roy was right and Sally was real. Eighty-four kilograms. Crap.

There was nothing for it; I'd have to try to lose weight. Like, *actual weight*. I took a good, hard look in the mirror. There was definitely more than one chin there. It was the same look I gave myself six months before I stopped drinking.

Is this how it's going to be every morning for the rest of your life?

The fuck it is.

So what now?

It was a very low point. I was tired. I was tired because I had two children under the age of four and a great but demanding job and I ate too much bread and chocolate and sobriety was still hard and cake made it better. And I was tired because this meant facing the truth that, as much as I told myself I was saving my family from a drunken wife and mother every time I filled the void with food instead of alcohol, really I was only kidding myself. There were never – nor would there ever be – enough ice creams, hot dogs, plates of chips with Thousand Island dressing, extra-thick shakes and lemon meringue pies to fill that void. It was bottomless. I was tired because I didn't think I had another concerted campaign left in me. I was sober and now I had to be thin. And being fat was awful, but the alternative – having to watch what I ate all the time the way I watched what I didn't drink all the time – seemed just as awful.

And still I didn't see it. I was trying to find my way across foreign terrain without a guide. I sat in the hole in my doughnut trying to eat my way out, not realising that with every bite, my clothes got tighter, until eventually the doughnut would be gone and all that would be left would be me. I would be my own doughnut. Argh.

When I stopped drinking I had known who to turn to for help, and slowly but surely I had built my own processes and management structure around myself, until I could cope on my own. Here, I didn't have anyone to show me the ropes.

Help came from an unexpected quarter. Lisa Raleigh burst into my life like a spandex-clad firecracker. She had just finished a stint on the South African version of *The Biggest Loser*. There had been no challenge too big and she attacked each one with the same amount of gusto that I attacked a bar of Cadbury Top Deck. *Great Expectations* was running a 'Booty Challenge' and I got a personal trainer and nutritionist rolled into one for eight weeks. The word 'competition' was what kick-started everything. When you try to better yourself you're like a hamster on a wheel; it doesn't matter how fast you go if you're only going nowhere. But when there's another hamster ... a different wheel.

I got Lisa, all blonde and tanned and determined. She was terrifying. I am still completely convinced that the Nutribullet was inspired by Lisa. She was a weapon of (my) mass destruction.

I didn't realise this at first sight. I met her at a health café in a vitamin emporium. Surrounded by zinc and magnesium and vitamins A through K, she changed my life.

"Right," I said confidently, "I'll do whatever it takes to win as long as it doesn't involve drugs."

And laughed.

Lisa didn't laugh.

"Oh, you'll win," she said equally confidently, "if you do everything I say."

How hard could it be?

"So what do we do first?" I asked happily.

"You do a seven-day detox. No coffee, sugar, wheat, dairy, meat, processed food, or alcohol."

"No coffee?"

That would be tough.

Her eyes iced over.

"No coffee."

Right.

"And I'll send you an exercise programme that will take 20 minutes a day. It mixes up—"

"Whoa! Twenty minutes *every* day?"

Ice again.

"Six days a week."

"Not a chance." I leaned back in my chair. "I don't have 20 minutes a day six times a week."

She eyed me coldly.

"Sam, *everyone* has 20 minutes a day."

"Not me," I said hotly. "I have a job and a husband and kids, and I don't have 20 minutes a day any day let alone six times a week."

Lisa was unmoved.

"And how many minutes a day do you think you spend sitting on the couch eating ice cream and feeling sorry for yourself?"

Wow.

"Okay, well that might be 20 minutes," I said meekly, feeling desperately sorry for myself.

She gave me a dazzling smile.

"Well, you can use those minutes then, can't you?" she said brightly.

And I did.

She made me buy things. Weights and rubber bands and a burst-resistant ball. I was a little insulted when she told me about the ball.

"I'm not *that* big," I smarted.

"I didn't say you were!"

"Well, why does my ball have to be burst resistant? It's not like I'm fat enough to burst it!"

She laughed.

"They're all burst resistant, Sam. Defensive much?"

I felt like a complete imposter walking into Sportsman's Warehouse and asking to be shown to the weights section. I'd never gone in any further than where the shoes were and that was right up front. There was a whole world past the racks of running leggings, a world I hadn't known existed.

I was very self-conscious buying weights. It felt a little like the first time I fooled around with a boy – you feel like you're supposed to know what you're doing, but you're not really sure. So, just as I did when I was 15, I pretended.

Looking as though I hadn't a care in the world, I tottered across the store, hauling two shopping baskets containing one each of five-, four-, three- and two-kilogram weights to the check-out queue. The cashier shook her head.

"There are trollies over there," she pointed.

Ah.

"Yes, I know," I said casually, patting at the vein that had popped out on my forehead, "I just felt like a workout."

Yeah, right. It was the Levi's Store all over again.

And so life became a workout. If I wasn't working out, I was recovering from working out. I do not remember being in that amount of pain since the anaesthetic wore off after my C-section. Gamely, I staggered to and from the gym six times a week to do my 20 minutes of torture. It was three days of cardio and three days of weights and every single one of those days was abs. Every. Single. Day.

The cardio was easy enough in that I knew how to use the running machine. Admittedly, up until the advent of Lisa, the highest setting I had used was six kilometres an hour. It was a nice little trot of a pace. The first thing to go was the word 'nice'.

"Two minutes at six, one minute at seven, one minute at eight, one minute at nine, one minute at 10 and then drop back down to seven," chirped Lisa over the phone.

"*Drop back down to seven*," I protested. "That's higher than my walking pace now!"

Lisa had a heart of stone.

"Do you want to win or not?" she demanded.

I did want to win.

"Then accept it. Your body will get used to it very quickly, you'll see! Anyway, repeat that until the last two minutes and then take it up to 11."

Eleven. Or, as I like to call it, fleeing from the police pace.

My body did not get used to it very quickly. Not for two weeks. That sounds very quick to some people. There was not a muscle in my body that agreed.

"Don't touch me," I'd groan pathetically as Martin tried to hug me in bed. "I want to die."

He looked worried.

"You sure you're not overdoing it?"

No, I wasn't sure, but I was going to carry on nevertheless. Something had clicked over in me. A switch had been flicked. Slowly but surely I got more and more excited about going to gym. The food was a bore, but the exercise was not. I finally understood the kick of endorphins serial exercisers tend to go on and on about. The first two weeks were dreadful, of course. Parts of me hurt that I didn't know I had. But after a fortnight I could do all 20 minutes on the treadmill. Including being able to flee the police, albeit only for one minute.

I would find a quiet corner of the stretching mat to do my stomach exercises. Tucked away behind the medicine balls and sandbags, I would crunch and pulse away for half an hour, taking little breaks to spy on people who seemed to be at ease using the machines.

Oh, the machines. I may as well have been asked to reconfigure a mainframe as to decode how they worked. Sometimes I would get lucky and a personal trainer chatting to a client would readjust everything very slowly, giving me time to try to memorise the order of actions. Pull that pin out, twist this, that bit adjusts the seat, that bit releases the weight. I didn't want to be one of those novices reading the directions off the side of the machine.

I also discovered a new-found discipline at home. I recorded all my favourite television programmes and only allowed myself to watch when I was bouncing up and down on a bosu, a sort of half-resistant ball on a little circle of plastic. Like a latex biscuit really. I lunged in front of *CSI*, squatted during *Who Wants to Be a Millionaire?* I did biceps, triceps and whyceps, muscles I couldn't see but which were apparently very important.

I found weights and lost weight. I lost lots of weight. I lost six kilograms in eight weeks, and I did win the challenge. I won by miles. And I was hooked. I had something that hit the spot almost better – and sometimes indeed better – than ice cream. I asked Lisa for more and more to do, and the more she gave me the hungrier I was. I ran on the treadmill. I even cycled, although I hated that. But fitness overtook me. Nothing in moderation, even now. Training was everything. I wanted to get better and fitter. And I did. I really did. And I lost weight. A magazine did an article about it. Then another one. How I lost *all* the weight. I was only seven kilograms above goal weight – my goal, not anybody else's. And I was still sober. I bought pants that didn't have elasticated waists. I fitted into the Levi's that had been in my cupboard so long they were practically vintage. I went to work at *Great Expectations* and the same clothes that had prompted Roy into his honest if unpleasant comment were no longer snug. In fact, they were so loose that I asked the production team if they could buy me more.

"We can't, I'm afraid," said producer Sharon apologetically.

"Why not? These are huge!"

As much pride as I took from being so much slimmer, that same amount of pride disappeared when I had to walk from the green room to the studio clutching the waistline of my pants so they didn't fall down.

"Budgets."

"Ah."

You only need to use the word 'budgets' in a can't-do situation. It's self-explanatory. But that didn't help.

"So what shall we do? I'm swimming in these!"

My wraparound top was now wrapped so far around my body that I had to tie it at the front instead of at the back.

"Well, I suppose we could staple you into them," she said doubtfully. "If we're careful, it should be all right."

And so that is what we did. Although I did have to wait until the last minute with my pants because once I was stapled in, any bathroom break had to be taken under the supervision of whomever had the staple remover that day. They couldn't have me tearing threads. My trousers thus had a bodyguard. Humiliating, yet effective. And I looked nice on TV. Everybody said so. And I was happier.

I had it all back under control, I thought.

But looking after yourself is like being a parent, always in charge, never in control. I was as much in control of my weight and fitness as I had been in control with my drinking. So I relaxed the 24-hour vigilance. And then, as gym got easier, the weight began to creep back up. Not a lot – a kilogram there, half a kilo up, half a kilo down. Finally, it steadied at around 75. I still weighed less than I had when I had had the kids, but it was still more than I liked. And, in frustration, I began to offset my workouts with chocolate and ice cream again. It was nothing for me to go and work out for an hour and then buy a slab of chocolate on the way home and finish it before I pulled into the garage. I was angry and irritable and I didn't know why. The excessive consumption had started again.

I tried another eating programme. When I started losing weight, a regime of restricted calorie intake was called a diet. A decade later 'diet' was a dirty word and the same thing was called an 'eating plan' or a 'lifestyle programme'. This one was pretty Spartan and boring during the week in terms of food choice (although there were liberal quantities of it), but offered a cheat day. A glorious, wonderful cheat day. A day when I was actively encouraged to eat as much as I could. It was an addict's dream. There was no ceiling but your own capacity. I don't think the idea was for followers to eat until they were sick, but I did. I ate pizza and chocolate and cheese. I followed the addicts' philosophy: it's not over until it's over, whether it was a bottle of wine or a carton of ice cream. Nowadays I try to buy ice cream in only half-litre increments. I know from experience that I will eat anything bigger than that in exactly the same time it will take for the former. *Why leave anything in the bottle? Finish what you start.* The same theory applied to everything. I would eat sugar until my hands shook and my heart pounded. I would eat until I was uncomfortable and then nauseous, and I wouldn't stop, even if there were two spoonsful or two squares or two blocks or two slices. I'd force down whatever was left with a strange desperation. It had to be finished. It had to be a clean plate, a clean slate, no matter what the consequence. If there was anything left, I couldn't be sure I wouldn't go back to it later.

That diet worked for a while too. I think it was the warped balance of deprivation and excess. It was the B-side to the drinking album. If I was 'good' during the week, I deserved the weekend binge. I'd earned it, like I'd earned a bottle of wine on a tough day. And just as I had eventually blurred the rules for my drinking – how it was every night, how it was more than a few glasses – I blurred the rules here too. I cheated once a week besides cheat day. Fruit wasn't allowed during the week, but I ate it because it was fruit. How could fruit be bad for me? And I paved my road to hell with bananas, grapes and apples. And I put on weight and complained bitterly, never acknowledging my complicity in the failure of the task.

Again and again, I sabotaged myself. Back then, I didn't understand why. But I know *now*. It was depression and fear of the unknown. For ages the dream of what life would be like when I was thin had kept me going as though it was some fantasyland in which everything would go right. Magically. It wasn't. I was still me. Still anxious, still nervy, still depressed. Just ... smaller. And smaller was becoming bigger again. I was afraid that the end goal was so close. What would I do when I hit this goal weight? What if everything wasn't perfect? What would I do next? And what if that *next* was nothing? I've always been a good competitor; I'm a very poor winner. Thin wasn't the answer I had hoped it would be. I hoped that learning to eat right and look after myself would provide some epiphany for me. Look, I have this in hand. I can take care of myself. I control my own destiny. But I couldn't control my own destiny when I wasn't sure what that destiny was.

I did know that it wasn't explaining to other people what the magic bullet was for losing weight. How was I going to tell that story? "Well, I stopped drinking, started eating, stopped eating rubbish food, started working out, started eating rubbish food again *and* worked out ..." That wasn't inspiring; it was just confusing. So I told everyone, perfectly truthfully, that it was about eating less and eating better food and exercising more, but that really was just the tip of the iceberg. That's the diet cliché. If it was so easy it would work for everyone, and it doesn't. There are reasons why we overeat. Some of them are symptomatic of today's way of life. We eat on the run. A lot. Good food takes time to prepare and, depending on how organic and free range you want to go, it's often very expensive. Portion sizes in restaurants are ridiculous. The plates we eat off now are the same size my mother used on which to serve a full roast chicken and vegetables. A muffin is bigger than an adult's clenched fist. You're doomed, from the time you sit down, to be fed like a goose that's about to become pâté.

But that's not why I ate. And I don't think it's why many people are overweight. I ate because I was tired and because I'd had a bad day and because I'd had a good day and because I deserved a break and because there was something good on TV. I ate malva pudding and custard when it was cold outside, and ice cream because it was hot outside, and everything else because it was there. And I ate because it was comforting, because it was the only time I felt like I was doing something for myself, however warped that may appear. Look how I would reward myself with a slab of chocolate: I would think, I've just run for an hour on the treadmill so I deserve it. I also deserved it if I'd been stuck in traffic or if I just wanted it. There was always a reason – the same way there was always a reason for a drink.

I didn't even see the parallels, although looking back they were as loud and as big as a digital billboard on the freeway, warning about traffic blockages ahead.

And so there I was, back in the queue for Skinny Club, and then it all changed.

"Why don't you try training to *do* something, instead of to *be* something?"

A trainer asked me that at the coffee shop at the gym.

But what would I do? I wondered.

I had never been sporty. Ever. In fact, the most energy I expended during most of my school sports history was on working out how not to do school sports. My school offered netball, tennis, hockey and swimming. I was bad at at least three of them. Really bad. I wasn't 'below average' or of 'could do better' standard. I was just bad. In netball I was the last to be picked without fail. It was pretty demoralising, but I didn't blame the team captains. I wouldn't have picked me either. I couldn't pivot without falling over. I couldn't score a goal. When I threw, I threw wide. I was very thrown by how some of my sweet quiet friends turned into Amazon warrior princesses on the court, their faces contorted with concentration, barking orders and throwing up their hands in frustration. That part, especially, would send me into a panic. How could someone who sat with me at break and swapped stickers and floral notepaper be swearing and screaming at me an hour later? Most disconcerting.

Then there was tennis. Jesus wept. The school tennis courts sat parallel to the church. To this day I think I am the only person ever to hit a tennis ball through an open church window by accident. And it was an accident, because, trust me, I could never have done that if I had been trying. The tennis coach was exasperated in the extreme.

"Sam, try to keep your eye on the ball!" he barked.

"I am! I am!" And I'd really try, but the racquet and the ball seldom made any kind of meaningful connection. On the rare occasion that it did, I don't know which of us was more surprised, him or I.

"That's great, Sam!" He would be giddy with relief! "Now just do it like that the next time!"

And I would go to the back of the line, even more anxious than before, wondering what I had done differently and how I would replicate a lucky fluke. And then I would miss the ball again and we would both sigh.

Hockey was worse. Hockey was so much worse. The coach was a wiry spitfire who had no patience with someone who had the ball sense of a strawberry. She called me Cowen.

"See how Cowen just did that?" she would demand of the class. "Now no one else do it like that!"

And I would be crushed.

It did, however, improve my negotiation skills. When we played an actual game, as opposed to a lesson of technique or punishment (usually dealt out for being late and involving running laps around the field), I would beg to play in right back position. I didn't know what right back was supposed to do besides defend the goal (we didn't have enough girls in the class for each team to have a goalie so right back doubled up), but I did know that if you were lucky, you could end up on the team made up of superior players who would keep the ball down the other end of the field, so there was almost no danger of me ever seeing any action. I just had to wander about looking as though I was excited by the possibility of involvement, and I was pretty good at that. It was nice and quiet up the winners' end of the field. It suited me perfectly.

This all changed if I was on the weaker team. Then the ball came at me time after time. And again and again I marvelled at how my lovely friends would tear down the field, their faces shiny and determined, ready to knock me flying to get a small hard ball between two posts.

"Cowen!"

Here we go.

"You barely defended."

Fair enough.

"That's twice! Twice you've let the ball through."

It was.

But.

"I don't know why you're just shouting at me," I would protest hotly. "It got through eight other people before it got to me! Why aren't you shouting at them?"

And once or twice that actually worked.

You had to play hockey unless you could prove you were doing two or more cultural extramurals a week. I did everything I could find. I did speech and drama. I joined the debating team. I even volunteered for the Johannesburg Junior City Council, which was its own story. On alternate Fridays I took the bus into Braamfontein and sat with a large group of 16- and 17-year-olds and discussed the city and how we could improve it. I don't think we did. I think there was talk of a concert or a festival or possibly a picnic, but that was it. And, quite honestly, I didn't care. I would have planted grass to watch it grow or painted stripes to watch them dry before I surrendered to hockey.

But then there was swimming. I liked swimming. I was not good at swimming, I hasten to add. I tried to be. It was the only sport for which I made an effort because I liked it and not because I was afraid of the consequences if I didn't. I enjoyed being in the water and I enjoyed the odd combination of camaraderie and solitude. I was slow and clumsy in the water, but I still liked it. In a class of 20-odd girls, you could hide in the water and just be happy. There was enough splashing going on to cover up any proper mistakes and, although there were so many of us, it was lovely and quiet under the surface. Just me, myself and I. I liked that. But I didn't think back then that I'd be swimming long distances in very cold seas 25 years later and loving it. I just looked forward to summer when there was no hockey and you only had to play tennis if you were in a team.

And then, after school, nothing. I joined the university gym and even went occasionally, but it was at the bottom of another campus and to walk back afterwards was all uphill, which seemed a bit of a sick joke, a workout after my workout. So, as you can see, exercise had never been a top priority for me.

Then fast forward 18 years.

And in a gym coffee shop it all changed again.

"Why don't you train for something specific?"

"Like what?"

"Like an event."

He was so casual about it. I wasn't. It was a completely foreign concept. He may as well have suggested I study medicine.

"What event would I do?"

He shrugged his shoulders.

"I don't know, a triathlon or a marathon or something."

Or something.

"I don't think I'm fit enough for that," I said cautiously. "Isn't that, like, years of training?"

He shook his head.

"I think you're fitter than you realise," he said, starting to unpack chicken breasts and brown rice and chopped vegetables. It looked as interesting as the leg of a chair. He ate that four times a day. "And you could start small. What about swimming?"

"What would I swim?"

I had horrible flashbacks of races and galas and school and being forced into doing the butterfly leg of the medley because I didn't put my hand up fast enough for breaststroke.

"What about the Midmar Mile?" he suggested. "That's coming up in a few months. That'll give you lots of time."

The Midmar Mile is the worlds' largest open-water swimming event. Thousands of swimmers, local and international, converge on the small KwaZulu-Natal town of Midmar every February and swim from one side of the Midmar Dam to the other. The event itself has been going since 1974 and now almost 15 000 swimmers compete every year, from professional open-water swimmers to youngsters in schools or with their parents, to seasoned veterans, to people like me, who want to see if they can swim what feels like a very long way through open water.

For me back then, sitting with the trainer in the gym coffee shop, a mile may as well have been 10 miles.

And yet ...

"Do you really think I could do it?" I asked doubtfully.

He washed down his chicken and rice with a protein shake.

"Yup. Just train for it."

So I decided that I would.

And the next day I started swimming.

PART 3

Swimming

CHAPTER 13

Hope floats

On 22 January 2014, at about lunchtime, I started to come round out of my first blackout in over 12 years to find myself face down on the bricks in the garden of the Big Bay Surf and Lifesaving Club. My first thought was of how uncomfortably familiar it all was. My mouth was dry, my body hurt, especially my head, and I had no idea where I was or how I had got there. Two of my closest friends were sitting on the ground next to me, watching me in silence, eyes wide and faces grim. I was sprawled on a square of grass between the showers and the clubhouse. The smell of vomit lingered in the air and I knew it was mine because I could feel the acid burn at the back of my throat and taste it in my mouth. I pulled myself up on to my elbows and threw up again. In a state of undress, people looking concerned, me on the floor without a clue how I got there. It felt so horribly familiar. But this blackout wasn't alcohol induced. I had hypothermia. It was the messy end to the longest swim I had ever done, the 7.5-kilometre swim from Robben Island to Bloubergstrand.

I owe my dedication to long-distance swimming to another form of exercise entirely. Between running and swimming, I fell into bikram yoga. A few people in recovery had recommended yoga as a gentle form of therapeutic help during the first few years of sobriety, but I had dismissed it out of hand. I was fat. The yoga I had seen in magazines and on television and even on social media was all being performed by men and women with perfect bodies who could twist and turn, and fold themselves into wonderful and impossible shapes and poses they could hold for ages. I couldn't even touch my toes. Yoga seemed a step too far – several steps too far. I didn't see how anything that made me feel that inadequate could possibly make me feel any better. I'd be the elephant in a tutu. So I didn't go.

How I ended up agreeing to sweating in a room of 68 people in 40-degree heat for 90 minutes I will never quite understand. I know it was because a friend was going and wanted company. I know I was curious; I'd lost enough weight by then not to be embarrassed about the way I looked in gym clothes. And it was years later. Many years later. A decade later. How hard could it be?

Hard. Very hard.

Bikram yoga is a series of 26 yoga postures and two breathing exercises that take place over an hour and a half in a hot room. A very hot room. Within minutes of arriving I wanted to leave. Or faint. Or throw up. Even when there are only a few people in the studio it can be claustrophobic and, with the number there were that day, it was downright unpleasant within minutes. One girl was finished before she started. Two postures in, she whimpered and made a dash for the door.

"Just try and stay." The instructor was a pint-sized woman called Zoey.

"I can't," the girl was gasping. "I'm going to be sick."

Zoey shook her head and smiled.

"You're not going to be sick. If you have the breath and the energy to say you are going to be sick, you won't be sick. If you were going to be sick you would have been sick already."

I sat on my mat on the floor, waves of nausea wafting over me and wondered how true that was.

"Please," begged the girl. "I need to get out!"

"I won't stop you," said Zoey. "But this isn't supposed to be easy. It's only supposed to *be*."

There were a lot of newcomers to the class. She addressed all of us.

"The purpose of this is not to do all the postures. The purpose is to stay in the room for 90 minutes. To try and stay. Sometimes that will be the most difficult part. Just to stay."

She was right. I hated every minute of that class. I swore I would never go back. I signed up a week later. Bikram was the perfect mix of suffering and success. Unlike other yoga classes, where the progress and choreography of the class was up to the instructor, bikram was rigid. The sequence never changed. The heat never changed. Dizziness and nausea came in waves, but so did euphoria. With every posture came awareness and understanding. Some evenings I would walk into class exhausted from the day and hit my mark in every pose. Some days I would walk in ready for perfection and lose my balance over and over again. The body always knew more than my mind. And I always went back; in fact, the days I felt like it least were always the days I needed it most. It calmed my mind. It is impossible to worry about lost passports and strange knocking noises in the car and whether or not I am a good mother when I am flat on my stomach on a mat, gripping my ankles and arching my back. I would go back to the AA mantra of 'Just for today'.

'*Just for today*, I will have a programme. I may not follow it exactly, but I will have it. I will save myself from two pests: hurry and indecision.'

At yoga, there was no hurry, no indecision. You couldn't rush through it like you could a gym programme, or modify it to suit your mood. There was a programme and there was tremendous comfort in following it exactly.

'*Just for today*, I will have a quiet half-hour all by myself, and relax. During this half-hour, sometime, I will try to get a better perspective of my life.'

It wasn't half an hour, it was 90 minutes, and from the outside it didn't seem relaxing at all. But while my muscles screamed at me, my mind unwound slowly, slowly and it gave me peace. It was – it is – a genuine peace. It didn't come from alcohol or theobromine and sugar. It came from within, which meant it was possible. It was success born of suffering, and it was worth it. However difficult it seemed on the day, I never left. Not once. Not when my legs were trembling and my shoulders were burning and the sweat ran down my back and my arms and dripped off my fingers. Not even in a class where I lay on the floor in corpse pose for half of it. I never left. The intention was always to stay. Or at least to try and stay.

I took that mantra to swimming. From purification by heat to purification by water. I have a black-and-white photo on my phone, the silhouette of a runner on a road and those words across the screen, 'It pains me to continue but it hurts much worse to stop.' These words encapsulated my mental state for as long as I could remember. There had never been any quiet time that wasn't substance induced. If I wasn't hiding behind an alcohol-fuelled haze, I was insulated by fat like the filling in a Cadbury crème egg. I was always looking for something that slowed down the main processor. I couldn't slow it down for myself; I never found the Off button.

My love for distance swimming was born out of Zoey's mantra, *Just try and stay*. I wasn't, and still am not, a natural swimmer. I'm not very fast or very elegant. No one will ever point me out and coo, "Ooh, *that's* how I want to swim." But I can swim for long periods of time at a consistent pace.

That first Midmar Mile was to redirect my attention. It reset my charge from negative to positive. The trainer was right: instead of working to lose, I was working to gain. And yet it wasn't my first Midmar Mile that caused that shift in me. No, I swam that one to see if I could. And I could. And I liked it because it made me feel strong.

Swimming was like finding a best friend. One that understood my limitations, but was happy to wait for me to catch up and love me through it. Even alone in the water, I came back time after time to the CS Lewis quote that had struck me the first year of AA. "*Friendship is born at that moment when one person says to another: 'What! You too? I thought I was the only one.'*"

I returned to swimming two years after my first Midmar Mile. It was born out of necessity and pain. I started swimming because I needed a form of physical activity that didn't involve working out in a gym. Because I own a gym. A bit of one. It was going to be an exciting and brave new adventure, but it didn't turn out that way for me. Sometimes I wake up at night in a chemical panic and my mind looks for something to hang it on and that is the first thing to shoot its hand up and say, "Pick me! Pick me!"

But every squat rack has a silver lining and mine was that the gym had no pool. So while I couldn't really train elsewhere, I could swim. Anywhere. Everywhere. No conflict. No irritation. No need to explain anything to anyone. No justification. So I swam in the pool of another gym. And it was lovely. And it was lovely every time. There was never a bad date. Like a perfect friend. Welcoming, available and warm. And I swam and swam and swam. Just a little at first. Maybe 10 lengths and then a breather. And soon – very soon, actually – the 10 became 20, then 40, then 80. And that was a mile. I was back in the game. And that was the key that unlocked the door to a whole new world of can-do.

And for the first time in ages, I was good at something I loved. Not *really* good. Not any kind of *golden mean* good. But good enough to attend little swimming events and not be last.

And, like drinking, like sobriety, swimming was a marvellous leveller. The first event I swam was at Germiston Lake and there must have been about 50 women in our category. As I was standing knee deep in mud and reeds, waiting for the start, I was knocked over by a much larger woman pushing past me to get closer to the front.

"Ag, sorry, my skat," she said, turning back and offering me a huge hand to pull me back to my feet. She was much older than me, in a swimming costume that wouldn't have been out of place in a fifties' beach scene. It was cut low on the legs and had a built-in bra, her breasts so high that she looked like the figurehead on a ship. As she hauled me up, her upper-arm fat wobbled.

"No worries," I smiled, and watched her waddle and then wade to the front of the line. Even as I thanked her, I was smug.

I would overtake her easily, I thought. It doesn't matter how far in front of me she starts, I thought. When the race started she launched forward into breaststroke. And she left me in her wake. By the time I rounded the first buoy she was past the second. She wore a bright pink cap with flowers so I couldn't miss her, even among all the other bobbing heads. When I eventually staggered out of the water, she was standing at the side of the finish holding a boerewors roll in one hand and a Coke in the other.

"Well done!" she called.

"Thanks," I cringed.

And I was never that arrogant again.

From my own experience, I should have remembered that you can never tell what's going on underneath the surface of someone else's life. We may look as though it's all smooth sailing, but, like a duck, you can't see what's propelling the motion from under the water. Even stripped almost naked, we are still unknown quantities. Swimming taught me that over and over again.

And with every little event, every extra length, I got good enough to swim for kilometres at a time and feel exhilarated instead of tired. I got good enough to let myself wonder what else I could do.

And with that came the pure and unadulterated joy of open-air swimming. Because gym pools are warm and sweet and comforting, and afterwards there are hot showers and fluffy towels and mirrors everywhere you look. But the truth is that it was like training wheels on a bike all over again. Once I was comfortable there, I could look elsewhere – and I did, I really did. Those weekend swims in local dams and lakes were soul food, swimming under the sun, in water that smelled different and tasted different and looked different. It wasn't always clean but it was full of life. The gym was clean and sterile and … dead.

And that's when the gift that was Zoo Lake public pool was given to me by my friend, Graham. And what a gift it was. I'd never considered using a public pool. The only one I had ever swum in was the one under the Summit Club in Hillbrow, one of the city's first strip clubs. A boyfriend played underwater hockey there and sometimes I would swim while they played. Even undercover, that pool was alive as well. There was a proper kaleidoscope of people, from kids learning to swim, bouncing up and down in the shallow end in shiny-eyed joy, to regulars who slipped into the same lanes and swam the same easy stroke, to the old men and ladies who would bob up and down aimlessly in the end lanes, like flotsam on the ocean surface. When we left with our wet hair and kitbags, there would always be a queue to get into the Summit Club, and there would sometimes be a concerned murmur from club goers as to whether they had missed the show, thinking we were the departing strippers.

But the Zoo Lake pool was different. It was recessed from the road so if you didn't know it was there you would miss it. A 30-by-30-metre pool with old-fashioned changing rooms, with wooden swing doors and a footbath to clean your feet before getting into the pool.

I constantly pinched myself that for R190 for a season ticket, I could go there anytime I wanted, on any day I liked, and swim in this square of liquid love. And there was never a bad time. Sure, in the heat of a weekend day, the pool was full of kids, but I could lie on the grass and talk about the meaning of life and love and whether the woman behind the bush to the right should really be wearing a bikini that shade of orange or dating such an obviously younger man.

And one by one, as 5 pm drew closer, all those people would peel off home and the pool would be mine. And I could go up and down for miles. And sometimes I did. Sometimes, when the noise was too much and when the sadness was too deep, I could go and wash it off. Over and over. Up and down. And I would swim into sunset and the water would ripple red and orange and I would swim into the darkness and sometimes the caretaker would forget to turn the floodlights on and I would swim in the dark water under the stars until 8 pm when the pool finally closed, and I would get out and everything would feel better.

And there were days when I went to the pool when I was happy too. I would go and swim simply because the day had been joyful. I'd made some money or seen a friend or played with the kids. Or just because the sun had been extra generous and the grass was extra green and those things just screamed out to be celebrated. And what better way to celebrate than to be right in there with them? In all the shine and the sparkle and the wetness.

That pool was its own addiction. I knew it. I knew it was ridiculous to drive double the distance it would otherwise be to the local gym where there would be secure parking and air conditioning and sparkling cleanliness and a pristine 25-metre pool, just so I could swim in a 30-metre pool, the length of which meant I had to count my lengths and work out afterwards – much like the posh jogging track – how far I had gone. And I would change in old-fashioned changing rooms with wooden swing doors and cold showers and an empty footbath.

Of course, that was the addict in me talking. And this time I let it. I knew swimming had tapped a nerve, but I also knew by now that I couldn't stop it. I'd always be an addict. I had fought it for such a long while. I so didn't want be one of *those* people, weakly lurching from booze to food. But over and over again, through years of denial and bargaining, I had had it slammed into my face that I am one of those people. And I can't fight the hunger. It is what it is. It's part of who I am. I can't be different. And water made that all right. That gnawing, gaping wound of need and insecurity that sucked me in like a black hole if I let my guard down even for a second … well, that closed over in the pool. Sometimes for a little while. Sometimes for ages. And no one got hurt. Least of all me. That was the best part. I got better and stronger and I worked parts of me I never knew I had. And I was sober. And I was not fat. And the after effects of a swim, unlike a drinking session or a sugar binge, were peace and calm. Like yoga, only better. I knew where I was and what I had done and that what the scale said the next day was immaterial. I was in love.

I took that love with me when I went back to Midmar. And this time Midmar was very special. Many of the smaller swims are on a triangle: you swim to one buoy, round it on the right, round the next one on the right and you end up at the finish, where you started. Midmar is different. You slip into the water at one side of the dam and you come out on the other. It's a journey where the start point is different to the end point. It's the place I went into the water knowing one thing about myself and came out knowing much, much more. And I liked that a lot. There were thousands of people there; there are thousands every year. But unless you are aiming for a fast time, if you swim off to the left of the pack, it feels like it's really only a few of you in the water. So I would swim off to the left, probably to the despair of the lifesavers and paddlers who would sternly point me back towards the main school of fish, and I would hear my own breathing, and the noise my own arms and legs made in the water and swim to my own time. And if I got to the end in under 40 minutes I considered that a win. Midmar brings together everything I hate and makes me love it. There are too many people, but the camaraderie is warm and real. There is a lot of noise, but I can tune it out. I am on my own in a cast of a thousand extras.

Midmar wasn't just a mile in open water; it was a mile through my soul. It showed me there was no end to the things I could learn and the places I could go. That there were new doors I hadn't seen and I could open all of them. And suddenly I wasn't in a transit lounge watching other people go to amazing places and do amazing things; I was going there and doing them myself.

It all sounds very silly, I know. It's probably why I didn't talk about it like this to many people. It sounds a bit like a crackpot religion. But it was, in a way. Because God was so very certainly in the water. So many times. Philosopher Alan Watts once said, "To have faith is to trust yourself to the water. When you swim you don't grab hold of the water, because if you do you will sink and drown. Instead you relax, and float."

There's always so *much* of life, and it always happens so loudly. But not in the water.

I got so sunburnt in those swimming days, but it seemed such an insignificant side effect compared to a hangover or a groaning scale. I looked like a reverse Top Deck, brown on my back and legs and shoulders and pale as milk on my thighs and shins and feet.

After Midmar came a three-kilometre swim in Bela-Bela, in a

beautiful dam surrounded by trees and scrub and wildlife, and yet it didn't satisfy me the way I thought it would. There were too many people; I wanted to swim by myself, which is impossible in a race no matter how slowly you are going. A woman nearby kept bumping into me, trying to head me off so she could clear the buoy before I did. I hated her. She was spoiling my swim. But it wasn't just her. I got to the end with a feeling that something was missing. It felt like a pizza with no cheese. I didn't know what it was but, even though I had never swum three kilometres before, it didn't make me tingle the way my first mile in open water had, and I drove home wondering if I could do something better or different.

Another swimmer I had met a few times told me about a five-kilometre swim I could train for, but instead of being excited, I was bored. I didn't want to swim around and around a dam. I wanted to do something else. And I was in the process of wondering how much more I could do and how much further I could go when along came a man I thought had all the answers. Along came Roger. And with Roger, the possibility of the biggest, best thing I had ever tried. Robben Island.

CHAPTER 14

Reach, pull, sweep

The first time I meet Roger Finch is at the pool. He is a short man with a year-long tan and a smile wide enough to split his face in half. He shambles down the steps with a cheeky grin. He has forgotten his swimming costume and wants to know if it's all right that he swims in his underpants. Caren – a fellow swimmer, lengths ahead of me in talent and experience – and I giggle at this sweet, affable man and agree that it is indeed all right. I think, well, if training is going to be like this, it'll just be fun all the time. I don't know Roger.

Roger has all the pedigree I could ever have imagined. He's swum hundreds of kilometres, maybe thousands. He's swum the English Channel and Catalina Channel and Rottnest Channel. Possibly the only channel he hasn't swum is a shopping channel. And he sees I've been swimming and wants to help. He sees in me something I haven't seen in myself. He see possibility in a woman who has no talent and no training but enormous determination. And I want to do something big. Something challenging. Something I can look back on and say, "I did that. And it was special." Robben Island to Blouberg. Seven and a half kilometres. Icy water. Only 500 people had ever done it. Ever.

And so I wrap up all my passion and determination in a towel and drag a dear friend along, and jump into a Ferrari going 200 kilometres an hour with no rear-view mirror – just as I had in my drinking years, as I had through my decade on a diet. And I am so excited and hopeful, that I forget why swimming is special. It is special because it is on my own terms, when so much of the rest of my life is not. All that calm, that peace, is mine – and, without realising it, I give it away.

My knuckles are white on the steering wheel on the drive to the pool. All the way to the pool. That's a long way to be tense. That's nearly 15 kilometres on a national highway. The temperature gauge in the car assures me that outside it is a balmy 12.5 degrees, but without the sun and with a nasty, vindictive little wind whipping the leaves on the grass verge up into random frenzies, I think it's much colder. In fact, I know it is.

Inside, the car is lovely and warm. I have hot air blowing in every direction, warming my feet, my legs, my face. I'm dressed in three layers of clothes. But I don't really feel the heat deep inside. All I can think about is how cold it's going to be when I get to the pool. How very cold and dark and overcast it will be.

There's a lump in my throat, and I'm very close to tears. As I take the Joe Slovo Drive off-ramp that brings me closer to my destination, my heart starts beating faster and faster. I try to talk myself out of it, out of the fear. I tell myself I want to do this. I say it's a journey and each step brings me closer to the goal. I try to imagine swimming in the sea off Robben Island, that freezing scream-it-to-the-heavens blue sea that looks so inviting. In the sun. Everything is better when the sun is out. But today … it isn't.

And today I am training with Roger. Roger, who hasn't swum for a week. Roger, who is going to watch every stroke. Roger, who will pick up on every lazy arm, on every time my arm doesn't reach as far forward as possible and follow all the way back through the water until my thumb grazes my thigh. He will see when I'm not kicking or when my right arm crosses the midline. And he will correct it. And I will be in the water and he won't.

I drive into the university. I'm not 100 per cent sure Roger is coming though, daring to hope. I mean, I told him I was going to be there at 1 pm, but he's been sick and he might not make it. And the covers might be on the pool and I don't know how to take them off by myself. And I don't have a key to the complex so I may not even be able to get in and then I won't be able to swim! And it won't be my fault! It won't be because I am scared and cold and slightly panicky about it being only me in the water, the slowest, the newest, the least likely to succeed on the wet road to Robben Island. It will be because of circumstances beyond my control. And then I can drive away, warm and smug in the knowledge that I didn't bunk a session. A Sign from the Universe that I should not swim today.

Roger's truck is in the car park.

I can see through the railings of the pool enclosure that the covers are off.

The door is open.

There's no escape.

I open the boot of the car and sit on the edge. I will not cry. *I. Will. Not. Cry.* I wanted to do this and I will do this. The Robben Island crossing will not swim itself. And I'm being a baby. It's one day. One cold, miserable day out of lots of sunny ones. And next week the others will be back; Caren will be back and she paces Roger, and my friend Graham will be better, and Swimming Barbie – so named because he has every accessory a swimmer could need – will actually arrive and Roger's focus will be split. And he won't get another opportunity to see exactly how little progress I've made and how slow and how new and how frightened I am. The spotlight will be off me. If I can fake it today, I'll be winning. So, with that less-than-convincing pep talk echoing in my head, I take my bags, and try to ignore the wind that's come up again and make my way into the sports building on campus.

It's almost as cold inside as out. I walk through the women's change rooms to the pool outside. I should stop and take my clothes off – I know that not to do so is just prolonging the agony, but it is *so* cold. And I am *so* tempted to run away. So I keep walking.

Outside the sun is making a half-hearted attempt to peer through the clouds. It's like an old lady behind lace curtains, twitching at them apathetically to see what the neighbours are up to. At the end of the pool is Roger, pulling up the thermometer. The thermometer that could, by half a degree either way, wither my already fragile resolve.

"How cold is it?" I ask him. My voice is very strong. It's not scared. The rest of me is scared, but my voice is not.

He smiles. He can. He's not getting in.

"Sixteen degrees."

Sixteen. It's 16. When we swam on Thursday, Graham and me, it was about 17. But it was warm outside. It was 21 degrees and the sun was there in full force, the life and soul of that pool party. The whole day was bathed in warmth. And every length and every stroke was loved by the sun. The cold water never had a chance to curl its icy fingers around our sense of purpose and pull us under. Today those fingers are much stronger; I can see them. There are little ripples on the water. They are waiting for me.

"So, what are we doing today?"

He smiles.

"Go and get changed and I'll tell you."

So now it's really happening. I am really going to get into that icy pool. I don't remember the last time I felt this sorry for myself. Every piece of warm, cosy clothing seems determined to hug me. I get caught in the sleeves of my pullover, I trip while I'm taking off my leggings. My Ugg boots have to be peeled off. Every piece of clothing is in cahoots to keep me dressed and warm. And all of them have to go. Eventually I'm shivering in a costume. My fingertips are numb, my feet are already starting to go yellow. I wrap my arms around myself, cap in hand and goggles over one arm, and run outside.

Roger eyes me disparagingly.

"Don't tense your arms. You'll only have to warm them up more."

Thanks, Roger. Thanks for that.

"So, what are we doing?"

I am determined to be cheerful. If I look cheerful I might actually be cheerful. And Roger is a gentle dictator, but a dictator nonetheless. As long as we're doing it his way, he's the nicest man alive. But there's no questioning the process or suggesting short cuts. Any of those have to come from him. I hope today that some come from him.

"I think we'll do Tuesday's programme."

Oh, great. I don't know Tuesday's programme. What the fuck is Tuesday's programme? Why would I know this? I just do what I'm told on this journey of cold and misery. Robben Island seems very far away today.

"Well, we'll start with a 500-metre warm up, then 400 hard, then 100 metres moderate, then 600 metres hard, then 100 metres moderate, then 800 metres hard and then 100 metres moderate ..."

It's like directions to a new place. And I've never been good at taking directions. After the third instruction I'm blank. I've got you for take the first right, the second left, go around the circle, but start telling me to turn left at the big tree and I'm long gone. Just like here. All I can hear is *hard* and *moderate* and bigger and bigger numbers. I keep nodding. Roger hasn't worked out yet that I'm not smiling any more. My face is in rictus and cannot move. It is frozen into place. For a brief moment I regret the botox in my forehead. I am physically incapable of wrinkling it to show how worried I am. I'm going to look relaxed no matter what he suggests.

"So that's supposed to be about four, but we'll see ... That might be too long in the pool."

Four. Yes, four. That's four kilometres. Two thirds of the way to my son's school. In a warm car. And a mean, little voice in my head says, *Yes, Sam, and that's only halfway across from Robben Island so if you can't do it now ...*

I go to the side of the pool. I won't put my foot in; I'll just get in. I'll get in straight away. I'll be really brave. That's what I'll be. I'll be really brave and proactive and ...

"Get in!"

Good old Roger. Doesn't mince his words. And, as if his voice was a magic flute, that breeze snakes round to lick the back of my knees with an icy tongue.

"I am. I will."

And I will. Very soon. Just after hell freezes over. Which should be very soon judging by the water temperature.

Roger isn't fooled. Or amused.

"You have a beautiful day here. You're really lucky."

"How," I ask hotly, "am I lucky? It's overcast, it's cold and there's a wind."

He shakes his head.

"There's no wind."

There *is* a wind. I can see the pool rippling. I tell him this.

"It could be worse."

"*How* could it be worse?"

He looks me straight in the eye.

"You could be wearing a lycra cap."

He's right – it could be worse. It could be torture. I had no idea the difference a silicone cap makes. Under Roger's tutelage, silicone caps only get a workout when the temperature drops below 18. It is like being offered an impossible choice: a lycra cap, which is horrible, over 18 degrees, which is nice, or a silicone cap, which is nice, under 18 degrees, which is horrible. For me it's the former. The sessions we did with lycra caps make my head ache in memory.

He shakes his head again.

"Get in."

I get in.

The cold hits me like a fist to the stomach. It knocks all the breath out of me. My bellybutton makes contact with my spine and stays there. I try to breathe out and can't. I look up at Roger. He's standing next to the diving block above me.

"Get going."

I can't even think about it. The cold has a vice grip on my toes, and my calves and thighs are burning. I think I had buttocks once, but I can't feel them now. I may have frozen my ass right off. I babble to Roger.

"Just give me a minute, just a minute, I won't be long, I won't need more, just a second to get used to it, just a few seconds ..."

He says nothing. Just extends an arm and points down the pool. And now there is no further respite.

I take one breath. One long, deep breath and drop down. Everyone else pushes off from the wall, but I don't do that. I drop, straight down, let that cold pull me under for a second and then I fight back. I extend my legs and push backwards as hard as I can. I feel my left calf threaten to lock and I ignore it. I'm in the water. I'm under. And I'm going through with it.

I don't breathe for the first 25 metres. I gasp. I flail. The cold tightens itself around my forehead and squeezes. It tries to get under my cap. Little icy fingers push at the sides of my head, gaining entrance where the hair is creating a pocket. But only a little. And not too far. The front of my face is a triangle of pain, from the top of my goggles to the seal of the cap. The whole stretch can't be more than five by three centimetres. But it can hurt 20 times that.

By 50 metres I get a rhythm going. I repeat to myself over and over: reach, pull, sweep. Reach, pull, sweep. Every time my arm emerges from the water it tingles. All the blood in my body is being pulled to the surface of my skin. By the time I turn again to get to 150 metres I feel more alive than I ever have. It's an endorphin rush second to none. There aren't enough Christmases and birthdays and lottery wins to make me tremble like this and still lunge forward. Reach, pull, sweep. My triceps are burning, my thighs feel hot as my thumbs graze past them, but they can't be hot. Can they?

I'm warmed up now. By 500 metres I'm ready for anything. Roger is sitting on the block, wrapped up warmly in a blue bomber jacket. He smiles at me. I smile too because I am so relieved. It's fine. It's okay. I'm warm. Well, I'm warm while I'm moving. So let's move.

"You were right," I say. "I am lucky."

He breaks into a grin.

"Now 400 hard."

And I launch myself off the wall to do 400 hard. And for about 200, it's all wonderful and fantastic and I'm the fastest, happiest little dolphin in the sea. And then ... I'm cold.

The cold sneaks up on you. You don't realise it's coming. That initial endorphin rush will carry you far. Well, it will carry me quite far. And when the sun is out, quite far can be miles. But the sun's not out. And the dark cold water is winning. Suddenly that arm that was flying out of the water needs a push. That swift head turn to the left or the right isn't swift enough not to take in mouthfuls of water.

I try to swim faster but the power isn't there. Cold makes me tired. I force it, though. I tell myself that if I can't do this, what can I do? If I don't have the mental strength to stay in a cold pool for more than 30 minutes, what kind of coward am I? I feel useless, like a waste of DNA – a timewaster, that's what I am. I am the reason that a man like Roger Finch, who has swum every important stretch of water in the entire world, by himself and after a broken pelvis, who has dragged himself out of bed where he has been sick for a whole week, has given his time, energy and heart to stand in the cold and watch me. How dare I not want to swim?

This takes me to the end of the *hard* 400 and the 100-metre recovery. Self-loathing is an easy default position for me. Maybe too easy. I've had years of practice. But I haven't had years of practice in the pool.

After the 100 metres, I cannot form words. Well, not so as anyone would understand. Roger laughs.

"Just relax," he says. "You're doing well."

He's such a nice man. Such a nice, kind man.

I clasp my hands together.

"*Don't do that!* You'll tense your muscles!"

Bastard. He is such a bastard.

Now it's 600 *hard*. And this is the lowest point in the pool I can remember. When Caren is alongside me, even though she is so fast and so good, I can feel her in the water. I can feel that energy, coming off another person, someone who is on the same path and has the same needs. And I can feed off it. I do it with Graham too, even with Swimming Barbie when he is there. I can be in their wake and swim through the shine and it sticks to me and warms me up and makes me faster and happier.

It is not there today. Today it is lonely and dark. I start to tear up in the water. In the cold, dark water. Every now and again the wind whips up again and slaps my arms or the backs of my legs. And it all conspires to say: You're not even halfway through the session. You've not even done two kilometres and you're wasted. You're finished. Your tank was never big enough to travel this distance.

I want to get out. I start trying to distract myself by counting lengths: 600 metres is 12 lengths. If I am on four lengths, then that's a third. Two more makes it half. Two more than that makes it two thirds. Then two more brings the total into double figures. Then two more and you're done. You're done. Then 100 slow. And I think about how I am going to do this swim in my head later, how I am going to couch it so I am honest but I don't scare myself or put myself off.

I don't let myself think about the 800 metres. It's a length at a time, 50 metres at a time. I look at the floor of the pool, so clean and clear. I count the lines on the bottom. First line across, I'm halfway; second, the start of the slope to the deep end; third line, the deep end.

I finish the 600. I'm exhausted. Physically and mentally exhausted. I'm going to say something. I've done 1.7 kilometres. It's not even half. If I feel this way before I'm halfway, I'm not ready to do this. The whole thing. Robben Island, all of it. I'm not ready for any of it.

And then the sun comes out. It bursts through the clouds with determination and force. It's suddenly so present and so strong, I wonder if it had been waiting for a cue. I wonder, in my warmth-deprived state, if it had been waiting for me to hit rock bottom before it stepped in. Sort of like a parent watching a child learn to walk and standing on the side lines waiting until a real fall is on the cards, and then swooping in to attend to any major bruises.

Roger is nodding on the side.

"You're coming on nicely, my girl," he says.

And I love Roger again. I love him dearly because when he says that I know I can do this swim. This session. And I can do *this* swim. This Robben Island crossing. This thing I think about in bed and when I am alone with a few minutes to busy myself doing nothing. And I know that I can do this thing because *he* knows that I can do this thing. And that one day I will be able to know it on my own. But right now, I need him to know it for me.

"Now 800 hard?"

I say it casually.

He nods.

I go.

And it's glorious. It's still cold, but the sun is warm on my back. It pulls my hips up when they threaten to dip under and change my head turn. It pours warmth into the air that I breathe in as I reach, pull and sweep. It's 16 lengths and I do count them, but each one is another exercise in stroke correction, not in my arms but in my head. Reaching, pulling and sweeping the joy back in. Of being kind to myself. Of believing that I can do this. That I *am* doing this. And I am frightened. And I am human. And that is all right.

CHAPTER 15

The island

It took a while to realise it, to realise that I had forgotten why I was there in the first place. The first few months of cold-water training were physically difficult but educational in the extreme. I corrected my stroke. I learned how to sprint – not well, but I did learn. I improved my form. I learned to tolerate cold water. And I lost a lot of weight, which, looking back, was quite important at the time. People, green with envy, would ask me what I was doing to lose weight and I would take considerable pleasure in telling them I was swimming up to 15 kilometres a week in sub-20 water temperatures. I wasn't going to offer anyone a short cut. Not if I didn't have one. And even though it was physically demanding, it was endurable. Because there was such a prize at the end.

But as the months went on and I got injured and recovered and reinjured and recovered, I lost my way. And the thing that had been mine was now Roger's. It was like a piece of antique furniture. If someone restores it, is it still yours? I went in green and eager and by the end I was strong and efficient in the water – and more anxious than I had been in years. I wanted to be good enough again. Again, in my own mind, I didn't measure up. I watched everyone else and fell further behind in my own confidence. I couldn't take pride in any improvement because it didn't feel like mine. Roger had pushed and encouraged and disciplined me into being a better swimmer. So did I have a right to be proud? Not really. Not any more. I went into the same spiral, the same loop I thought I had escaped, the one where I will never be good enough. Good enough for whom? Myself. Again and again I would say it to myself. What is enough? Just a little more. And the water, which had been my go-to place, was now my run-from place. Sometimes, on my way to the changing rooms, I would look longingly through the fence at the pool, the way I sometimes look at an unopened bottle of scotch, and wonder how I could go back to the way it was, or whether it was gone forever.

The day of the swim didn't start like that. The day was perfect. There was almost no wind. The temperature of the air was tracking a midday high of 30 or 31. The sea was calm, not a white horse to be seen. It was as though the ocean gods had got together with the air gods to promise the most beautiful day. This was the day Roger had planned for. He had waited and waited, and we had waited with him, for the perfect day. For months he had checked Windfinder, an app that gives you a seven-day forecast of wind and swell conditions. There had been tiny windows of opportunity starting in October, running through to the new year, but Roger was waiting for a gap of at least four days. And it came in the third week of January. All those months of training in the cold winter waters of the Wits pool had led to this morning, this moment, this swim. And he had got everything right. Except the water temperature.

We didn't know that; none of us did. On our way over to the island, the boat hit a bait ball. There were penguins and dolphins and seals swimming around and under the boat, all feeding as though they had never and would never eat again. Seabirds swooped down to fish, barely touching the surface of the water. It was a moment of pure happiness, watching all the sea life that makes up a microcosm of what is beneath the ocean surface. That happiness lasted a long way and a long time. It lasted the journey to the island, through getting into the water, through the swim to the rocks at the edge of the little pier, the one you barely see in postcards. Postcards are useless for perspective. You can only really get a proper feel for the distance of the swim from an aerial photo. I used a postcard to show my children how far I had swum, to show them what a feat it was. I suppose some part of me thought that if they were impressed then I could be as well.

They weren't.

"Did you go to the museum first?" Chris asked me excitedly.

"No, I swam from the edge of the island."

He was disappointed.

"But why didn't you go to Madiba's cell?"

"Because you don't actually go *on* to the island. You swim from the edge."

Didn't I just say that?

"Well, I think you missed an opportunity there," he said disparagingly.

My daughter was even more dismissive. She studied the postcard and asked, "Did you swim to the mountain?"

"No, I swam from the island to the shore on the left."

She inspected the shore on the left.

"You can't see the beach."

I had to agree with her that, indeed, you can't see the beach.

"Did you swim to Durban?"

"No, I swam to Bloubergstrand."

She looked at me, confused.

"But isn't that in Cape Town?"

"Kind of. Sort of."

"So basically you just swam from Cape Town to Cape Town?"

And that was that. They say children are a grounding experience. Mine ground me down to a paste.

I loved the swim for quite some time. I loved Roger, so sure and confident of the adventure, so certain in his natural habitat. I loved it until the time I thought my mind was playing tricks on me. Although the sun was out and there wasn't a cloud in the sky, the water seemed to be getting colder. I didn't ask anyone if it was and nobody had said anything. I just assumed it was me. But I knew what had been lovely was now becoming unpleasant.

I was getting scared because my head had started to hurt and that had never happened before, even an hour or two into a training session. My fingers were starting to separate and refused to come back together. And I was cold. I was achingly, miserably cold. I started to feel as though I was dreaming. Faces would come into sharp focus and then veer out again. The temperature of the water had dropped from 13.7 just off the island, which was cold but doable, to a fraction under 10 degrees offshore. It was the coldest water I had ever swum in; it was the last kilometre of the swim and I was very cold and very tired.

You can't tell how cold the water is when you look at it from the beach. Sometimes there's a clue: if you can see a long pale stretch in relief against the darker blue, that's going to be your cold stretch. But sometimes there isn't one. Sometimes you don't know until you are in the water and your ankles ache and your legs feel weak and you have an urge to sit, which is countered only by a stronger urge not to be waist deep in icy water. The cold isn't always matched by the weather. The coldest water I had encountered before that day was 10.5. That was off my favourite swimming beach, Clifton Fourth. The day was grey and clouds spat raindrops as I waded into the water, and I was shocked – physically and mentally – at the viciousness of the temperature. The beach is small and protected and there are lots of rocks to act as pointers and geography for when I swim off in the wrong direction, which I do often. But that day, even Clifton was unfriendly. That was cold like I had never experienced – cold that made me nauseous and hurt my head, and made it hard to draw breath – but as I kept swimming, my body fought back and I got warmer. In fact, for the 40 minutes I swam with Roger and my other swimming mate Caren I was on a bit of a high. It was like a million little burning needles stabbing my limbs, making my muscles twitch and work. Strangely pleasant. Very strangely. It was only later that the unpleasantness started, the fallout, the after effects. Even after towelling off, pulling on layer after layer of clothing and scrambling into a warm car to run the heater full blast – as I did after a training swim in the pool – I still shook for ages and my jaw clenched until it hurt. I had a renewed respect for hot chocolate, a drink I hadn't had since I was a girl, because sipping that for 20 minutes after getting out was like drinking some kind of magic. And eventually I got back to normal.

It doesn't sound like a lot of difference, 10.5 to 9.8 or 9.9, or whatever it was, but it felt like it. A seasoned swimmer, another Martin, told me that the difference between 10 degrees and 12 degrees is not the equivalent of the difference between 20 degrees and 22 degrees. Mine was apparently the coldest first-time swim on record. But it doesn't really matter. Because I don't remember it.

Other people have filled in the gaps for me. Apparently, a kilometre or so offshore my mind shut down. There's a view that your body will continue long after your mind has given up and I subscribe to that. I don't remember that last stretch of water. I don't remember telling Roger I was frightened, but it seems I did. I don't remember him telling me I would make it. I have a flash of yellow in my memory, perhaps gold. It's in my peripheral memory bank, because if I close my eyes and try to visualise it, it's gone. I couldn't see the buildings, although someone told me later that I had nodded when they had let me know. I remember Roger telling me to stand up, but I refused – I wouldn't give up. I had come too far and I could see the gold/yellow strip. He hauled me up and I was ankle deep in water. For all I know I could have swum myself into the sand.

A newspaper later carried a story on the swim. There's a picture of me, Roger on one side and Robben Island veteran Theo Yach on the other. By the time you read this book he will have done 100 crossings. I don't remember him being there at the end, but he was.

The next few hours are gone. I remember only brown tiles and more water. (The tiles were white and I was in a shower.) I know my friends held me up while ice swimmer Ram Barkai tried to talk me – and them – through hypothermia and how to deal with it. I didn't hear that, or someone offering me alcohol, which, luckily my friends refused for me otherwise I would have woken up in more trouble than I was in half-conscious. They rolled me onto the hot bricks outside, murmuring words of comfort, desperately trying to warm me up and bring me round. It was a long process, as much, if not more, for them than me. I woke up to throw up, distantly aware of a towel draped over my bottom. Later my friend Ryan told me he had done that because someone was taking photos. They were. Some of those photos ended up on twitter. That made me laugh. During my times of having drink-related blackouts after dancing on tables and passing out in my car, there had been no social media. Now here there was a picture preserved for the world to see of me throwing up on the grass with almost no clothes on and I had been 100 per cent sober.

The swim was over. Reaction was mixed. My husband was furious with me for risking my life and so was my mother. My father was bitterly proud. My colleagues were surprised and impressed.

"Sam, that's really far!"

I agreed weakly that it was indeed far. Really far.

"Weren't you afraid of sharks?"

"Nope. In my single days I dated enough of them ..."

I was such a nerd and I had done such an un-nerdlike thing.

But none of them know what it was like in the water. What it was like to wake up in despair knowing that that swim would never have succeeded if it weren't for Roger. That the signs all spelled danger and we just hit the accelerator. And that he was right. When the chips were down and it was a matter of survival, my gut instinct was to survive. Even if my mind had already given up. And that thought sometimes keeps me awake at night.

But I still thought, even after that, that Midmar could fix things again. Because it had fixed things before. So I entered and went down to swim. But I had forgotten how to swim just for the love of it. I couldn't just be in the dam watching the sun dance on the surface as I stroked my way through the water. I didn't think that would be enough. I would need something big to wipe out what had gone wrong. So I entered the eight-mile. The eight-mile is where swimmers take part in all eight of the mile-long events held over the two days. I was bruised and stretched, physically and mentally, but I was back in the loop. If I could do this next big thing I could forgive myself. I could let the Robben Island thing go. I could be merciful.

All the signs were there that things were not as they should be, that I was wildly out of equilibrium. I was obsessed with getting 'a time'. It had never mattered before. I was grasping for proof. I had a shoulder injury that had recurred for months and I ignored it, and the very real possibility of doing further damage. I had hurt it so stupidly. Months before Robben Island I was finishing a four-kilometre set when my right shoulder started to niggle. A normal person would have got out of the water. A normal person would have gone home and put ice on it, or a hot pack or taken an anti-inflammatory or called a physiotherapist. I did none of those. I stood shivering in the shallow end and asked myself how far, if I was in pain, I could go before I couldn't swim any more. Just as, years ago, I had asked myself how many bottles of wine I could drink before I passed out.

How much is enough? Just a little more.

I swam another 1300 metres before I stopped. During that time, my right arm went numb. It didn't stop me. The last 300 metres were punctuated by shooting pains through the top of my right arm, every few strokes. That didn't stop me either. It won't be that bad, I told myself. It'll hold until I get back to Johannesburg, I told myself. Just the same way I had told myself 12 years earlier that I would only drink two glasses of wine. That I would be absolutely fine to drive home. Just the same way I had eaten slab after slab of chocolate, day after day, promising myself that every single one would be the last one, the very last one. All lies, not just to others – to myself.

That injury had kept me out of the pool for weeks. It was a rotator cuff tendonopathy, but you could have called it a life sentence. Even though it was my own fault, I was unplayable. I was tense and edgy and irritable. I kept going back to swim before it had healed properly. I had a cortisone injection to reduce the inflammation. The doctor told me to stay out of the pool for 10 days. I was back in seven. I couldn't stay away. That pool may as well have been made of chocolate and filled with Merlot for the magnetism it held for me. It kept me out of the pool for a week here and a week there, but I had Robben Island in mind, and my shoulder was just going to have to learn to live with that.

At Midmar, though, I knew after the first mile that I should stop. I got into the water tired and I got out even more tired. I had no power. The engine needed a full overhaul and I knew it, but I had slapped on new tyres, done a quick paint job and hoped that would be enough. It wasn't. But I didn't stop. My friend Graham, who had also come down to swim the eight-mile and who swam like a fish, would be over the mat before me every time and watched me crawl out the water with ever-growing concern.

"You know you don't have to do this, right?" he said, worried.

I just raised my eyebrows at him. Of course I had to. He understood; good friends always do – not *why* I had to do it, but that I would. Still he tried to talk me out of doing the four miles the following day.

And, as nature is wont to do in these circumstances, the wind came up and the dam got choppy. It is a myth that inland waters don't have waves or pull. Each mile was more difficult than the last. I felt my shoulder grinding again and again. I had a picture in my head of two bones rubbing against each other. The pain was intense. I didn't stop. I was mad, crazy, sure I would be all right. I had been all right before.

I was not all right. I knew it, but Robben Island was there in my head. And I saw it in every mile, especially the third one, when the chop was so high and I couldn't see the end. And I swallowed so much water and I thought this must be what it feels like to drown. And that was a direct flashback. And it was terrible. But I swam on.

My poor shoulder, which had protested so vigorously and tried to protect me from the worst of my fears by slowing me down and diluting my training frequency, had just had enough. So it threw in the towel. It didn't want to prove a point or right a wrong. Robben Island was over. And that horrible feeling of failure should have been over too. That hunger to feel triumph again. But it wasn't. That shoulder wanted me to swim in the sun and get mildly burnt and eat Cadbury's mint Bubbly and be happy. It wanted me to remember that when I was a shit swimmer I was happy just to be in the water, and to let go of feeling I had anything else to prove to anyone. And I couldn't.

I got back to Johannesburg and went to see my physiotherapist and friend, Ryan. I couldn't even raise my arm without wincing. What followed was almost as traumatic for him as it was for me. As a professional, it is difficult to impart bad news. It is even more difficult when the patient is one of your closest friends. I sat on the bed in oversized rugby shorts and a backless gown and watched his face.

"You need to stay out of the water for a while." He said this gingerly.

He may as well have told me not to breathe.

"How long is a while?"

He was silent and then, "A while."

"A week?'

I could manage a week.

"A bit longer than that."

No.

"Two weeks?"

He didn't answer.

"Sam, if you go back to swimming right now you will be on an operating table in two months."

I burst into tears.

My poor, dear friend watched in awkward agony. He patted my shoulder. It's difficult to hug someone wearing a backless gown and rugby shorts. Even when you're friends.

Fallout. Again.

Like Martin watching me at the car.

Self-destruction is also a terrible spectator sport.

CHAPTER 16

The deep end

So swimming was over for a while. A long while. I felt like I had lost a friend, and had no idea where to look for him. That hole, that void was so much bigger now. And over that time, over weeks and weeks of running and rehab exercises and frustration, I wondered over and over how I missed the signs of it all going wrong. The only thing I was sure of was that if I could turn the wheel back – and of course hindsight is always 20/20 vision – I would swop being a better swimmer for being a happy one. Anytime. Every time. But it was too late.

I went down to Cape Town for the Two Oceans half-marathon later that year and I went to Clifton and stood in the water and I went to Camps Bay beach and ate ice cream and cried, but I didn't swim.

It was a long time before I was able to go to the pool on my own in that cold. I had clung to Roger's matter-of-fact confidence like a child on a bicycle about to give up her training wheels. When my dad was holding the back of my saddle as I wobbled along on two wheels, I could feed off his confidence. It was the same in the pool. When Roger dropped his thermometer into the pool and I watched it sink down into the water, it felt like my heart was going with it. And then he would pull it up and smile at it and my heart would come with it. It would be all right. And it always was.

When I went back on my own, it was a different story. My thermometer was a dolphin on a stick. It bobbed chirpily on the surface of the water. It didn't feel the cold, possibly because it couldn't drop under the surface and come back up with an ice-cream headache, a brain freeze. The temperature beneath the surface is quite different. An unheated pool is like a baked Alaska; there's the warmth of the surface followed by the shock cold of the middle. And in the sunshine, there is no warning. I went back to the pool in winter, five months after I stopped swimming completely. I had tried to swim short distances in the pool at the gym, so I'd essentially put the training wheels back on the bike. But my shoulder would throb within 100 metres and I would grow anxious and upset and get out.

Gentle Ryan tried to reassure me when I went to him again and again to look at it and prod around.

"It's fine, Sam."

"It doesn't feel fine."

"It's more in your head now."

And maybe it was. But it was there. So I stopped swimming in the gym pool and went back to where it had all started. In August, two days before my birthday, I went back to the pool at Wits College of Education and got into the water again.

Everything was the same, and yet everything was different. My thermometer was still a fish, but the dolphin thermometer was now a clownfish. The dolphin had suffered an untimely demise under someone's foot at the beach. The clownfish was just as bouncy in the water. The temperature was 15. I was overjoyed. And I swam. And my shoulder didn't hurt. And the next day I went back. And then the next. And I called Roger, who was about to help someone else do a long swim – the English Channel – and he was overjoyed too and said he would come swimming with me when he got back.

My solo pilgrimages to the pool all followed the same ritual: if it was sunny, I would drive there in happy denial, the brightness and cloudlessness of the sky belying the temperature on the thermometer on the dashboard. Who could believe it was 13 degrees outside when the sky was so blue and the sun so blinding?

The illusion would be shaken somewhat when I opened the car door in the almost empty car park on campus. When the air was still, it was pleasant, but then when it wasn't, a little winter wind would come and curl around my ankles and push icy fingers under my socks and down my neck.

The changing rooms were always cold. They had an institutional feeling of woe. The tiles were old and when I turned on the shower, water would spurt everywhere, years of limescale in the jets making for interesting patterns on the walls and the ceilings and almost anywhere in fact except on the shivering body underneath. I'd strip off, asking myself every minute what I was doing. Was it really this important? Yes, it was. Yes, it is.

Something always brought me back. As the temperature fell from 20 to 18, to 16, and then hovered between 12 and 14, I had to find reasons to push myself in the water. For a while there was Sarah. Sarah was tall and beautiful and at least 20 years my junior. She was a student who was teaching herself to swim. She had a bizarre ritual of taking a hot shower first and then jumping into the pool. When I first met her she couldn't swim 10 lengths without pulling herself along with her hands on the wall. She had a headful of dreads and her swimming cap used to sit on them like a silicone turban. She never wore goggles. I gave her a pair of mine; I was always experimenting with new goggles – I still do. I didn't realise what a lopsided face I had until I bought goggles. My left eye always has a permanent black shadow under it for the few months it takes me to manipulate the bridge of the goggles until it is flexible and more forgiving of my facial flaws.

I gave Sarah a pair to try. She gave them back half an hour later.

"Don't they fit?" I asked her. "'Cos, I have more if they don't?"

She shook her head.

"No, thank you. I don't like being able to see the bottom of the deep end."

The deep end is 3.5 metres deep. It's a very deep end indeed.

"But doesn't the chlorine and salt hurt your eyes?"

"Seeing the bottom is worse."

"Aren't you scared, not being able to see?"

She shook her head.

"If you can't see it, you can't be scared of it."

I wish that were true.

Sarah always brought me back to earth. One Saturday I was swimming with friends and the temperature was 13.8. When it first starts dropping, every point of every degree feels important. It was never 'between 13 and 14'. It was 13.8. And we were debating it.

"It's 14," protested Mike, a strapping six-foot-something swimmer who sends me weekly training programmes for new and different swims and puts me through my paces with ruthless love.

"It's 13.8," I was firm. It was my fish on a stick. I knew how to read him.

"Well, it looks like 14 to me."

"The mercury stuff isn't even touch—"

There was a huge splash and we both spun around. There was Sarah paddling determinedly towards the end of the pool. Sarah, who could swim 10 lengths slowly. Sarah, who had no heart-rate monitor and no goggles. Sarah, who refused to talk about it or worry about it or consider it. She just did it.

She had embarrassed us both.

So we quietly got in.

And swam three kilometres.

Sarah reminded us what swimming was about. It was about getting in and doing it.

In winter, I tried to swim during the day. Cold water heals a lot of injuries. Niggling shoulder problems disappear in a kilometre of cold water. Elbows, deltoids, triceps and pectoral muscles loosen up, and aches and pains fade away. After months of shoulder strapping and physiotherapy, it took two 45-minute sessions at 11 degrees off Clifton Fourth Beach to make it unnecessary. But it goes much deeper than that. Even in the coldest water the sunshine promised joy on its best day and solace on its worst.

CHAPTER 17

Surrender

When my mother died I swam out my grief every day. The day she died was the worst day of my life. When I was young, I had thrown that sentence out so casually. I remember getting a pimple on my face the night before my matric dance. I thought that was the worst day of life. Then a boy I thought I loved slept with another girl behind my back and I thought that was the worst day of my life. Sometimes the bathroom scale tipped over into dangerous territory and those were definitely the worst days of my life. But until my mother died, I had never fully appreciated the power of those six words: the worst day of my life. She was half of me, and when she died I felt as though half of everything I was had died with her.

She hadn't been well for a long time, but it was still a shock when she was gone. She was the biscuits in the tin and the birthday and Christmas cards on the dining-room table. She was the trifle on Christmas Eve and the laughter at lunch. She taught my children to play blackjack and cribbage and made me drive all over town to find the water tower Christopher wanted for his railway track so she could wrap it up and give it to him. She was a human pool noodle for my daughter. My son preferred spending time with her to spending time with me and was quite vocal about it. Months after she died he found a stack of postcards in a drawer that I had put there for him. She always sent postcards, from wherever she went. My mother didn't believe in computers and emails and texts. She had a pen and a postcard and a stamp and a post box, and with every picture she sent, she offered us a piece of her world. He howled in my arms for hours, my 12-year-old man-cub.

"Sometimes when you were late to pick us up from Grandma I was glad," he whispered. "Because I could be with her longer and more."

Genevieve was soft-heartedly practical. She tried desperately to help. She was bewildered by the extent of my tears. She was certain her grandmother was in heaven and no longer in pain, and in the face of that childlike certainty we lose as adults, she struggled with the depth and breadth of my grief. When I would come home from my father's house with things my mother had collected or put away for a rainy day, Gen would try to hide them in her room so I wouldn't have to look at them and be sad. I caught her dragging a whole suitcase down the hall.

"See, Mommy," she said, "I'll look after it until you stop crying."

It will be there a long time. I have not yet stopped crying.

When I came home the day I cleaned out my mother's cupboards I knelt on the floor of the garage and sobbed among suitcases and plastic bags full of her. She had kept everything; scented drawer liners, soaps, the old school books of all three of her children. I took everything I could carry. I couldn't bear to lose anything I could remember her loving or wearing or 'saving'. My mother 'saved' a lot of things. I don't know why. I slept for months with a shawl she had worn a lot when I was little. It was dark green and had little bits of glitter in it and she wore it in the evenings when she was cold.

All children have a healthy sense of acquisition and my own both ask me regularly if they can have my things when I am dead. I asked my mother about that shawl, if I could have it when she was dead. And now she is dead and I have it. And however tightly I wrap it around myself, it will never be as warm as being held by her.

I can't use the word 'lost'. I didn't correct people when they said, "Sorry you lost your mother," but I wanted to cry, "I didn't *lose* her! I know where she is. She was taken from me." She loved birds. She fed the ones in her garden twice a day, once in the morning and again in the late afternoon. She had hanging trays for the loeries and mousebirds and barbets, and she would cut up apples and bananas and pawpaw to fill them, and when she did that she would fill the seed dispensers she had for the weaver birds and red bishops and sparrows. The day after she died, I stood in her living room, looking through the window into the garden at those bird feeders. The big, awkward fruit-eating loeries swung on their table, pecking at the bottom of the tray. There was no fruit that day. I wondered if they would realise she was never coming back.

I thought about those birds often, looking lost on the feeder that she no longer filled. They were lost. She was dead. I put her clothes in bags, and sealed them with sticky tape, wrapping it around and around the plastic in an attempt to keep her smell locked up for in case. In case I needed her. At 42, there was still enough of the bereft child to hope that if it got too much to bear, if the pain was too heavy, I could tear open a bag and wrap her jacket or her sweater around me and breathe her in. I don't know if it will work; I don't know if I have wrapped the bundle tightly enough. But perhaps I have and there are little packets of her that I will have in reserve. I hope so. I need it to be so. She was the safest of safe spaces.

The pool became the next best thing. In the pool I swam and swam. It was the only place I could remember her and not cry. You can't cry in goggles – it's physically impossible. I don't know why. In the pool, I could feel her hug and I could hear her laugh and I could see her, my brave beautiful mother, who fought cancer so many times and refused to let it change how she lived.

During her first bout of chemotherapy, I bought her an artwork by Hannah Lurie titled *I'm Too Sexy for My Hair*. It was a plaster head with bright make-up: eye-shadow, blush and eyeliner, and a dash of red lipstick. My mother loved it. She was it. She put on make-up every day. She went to chemotherapy with her eyebrows painted in. She wouldn't have been caught dead in a tracksuit. Literally. No matter how sick the drugs made her, she was determined to stay herself – and she did. I was in awe of her.

When she was gone I found myself drowning in the void she had left. Mike would send me training sessions of two- and three-kilometre stretches, and sometimes I would overshoot them until my shoulders hurt and my fingers separated and my feet were numb and then I could get out. If I was physically numb, sometimes I could be emotionally numb as well.

God always sent me something in the water. Most often it was sunshine and the promise of a wonderful sunset. A sunset can change everything; for an hour I could turn my head at the end of every length and watch the light glint on the golden statue of the trumpet-blowing Angel Moroni on the white-tipped towers of the church of the Latter Day Saints further down on the Parktown Ridge. Over the wall at the end of the pool there were four trees that varied in size and seemed to have decided to arrange themselves from biggest to smallest in order of appearance. The sun would sit on top of the tallest tree for what seemed like ages, like a child at the top of a slide, holding on for dear life. And then, just as a child lets go, the sun would slide down the other three trees and pause briefly to bathe the angel in light, and then it would drop and so would the outside temperature by at least two degrees. Ironically, that pushed me harder. The colder it got, the faster I swam.

I'd always get in while the sun was still high. First I would check the temperature, no matter what. Whether the wind was whistling and the clouds were blanketing the sky or the sun was defiantly ignoring winter and the water was shimmering, I took the temperature. I had to know. It was its own form of control. If I had the information I would know what to do. Perhaps it is more accurate to say that checking the temperature gave the illusion of control. Deep down inside I had no plan to do anything but swim. No matter how cold the pool, I never walked away. It wasn't in me to do it. I knew that if I let myself walk away once, the door would be open for me to do it again. Like a glass of wine. If I drink one once, there will be another. Is it definite? No. But it's definitely a maybe, a probable even.

Then I would sit on the side with my legs in the water. Some swimmers advocate jumping in – the shock is brutal, but it's mercifully fast – but I am not in that club. I prolonged my experience, letting first my ankles, then my calves ache until they stopped. I would unpack my wet bag, the mesh bag a lot of swimmers carry. I'd place my fins and my pool buoy and my hand paddles on the side of the pool. If there was a wind, I would arrange everything so the soft, light foam of the pool buoy was under a pyramid of fins and paddles, in case it blew away. I didn't want to have to get out and retrieve it if it did. I didn't think I would have the mental strength to get back in once I was out of the pool. Especially if it was getting dark. Then the water stopped being welcoming and became forbidding. Come on then, it said, see how far you get.

Eventually, it would be time. I would ease myself into the water up to my ribs, swearing all the way.

"Fuck! Fuck! Fuck! Fuck! Fuck!"

My whole body would hate me. Roger used to tell me not to stand on tiptoe in the pool.

"What are you doing that for? Stand flat. You're going to get wet anyway!"

There were no short cuts or easy outs with Roger. He pushed himself as hard as he could and he had no patience for cowards. And tiptoe was cowardly.

But on my own I was on tiptoe so high I was practically en pointe.

Once or twice I smacked the water. But not in front of Sarah. Never in front of Sarah. Sarah made me want to be a better person. So there would be no slapping.

Then there was a countdown. I waited for my thighs to burn. As soon as the burn started I knew I would be all right. The colder the water, the quicker my legs heated up, that strange feeling that crawled from the back of my knees, around to my quadriceps and gripped them. Then it was time. So I would do the drop down, straight down like a stone, and then push off from the wall, swearing quietly to myself all the way.

No matter how often I did it, I was never prepared for the shock of the cold. Sometimes, if I had eaten too recently beforehand, the food would force its way back up and I would have to force it back down before it hit the water. The triangle of pain would hit my forehead like a brick and I would gasp from side to side instead of breathe. And every time I would hate it for 50 metres and, on especially cold days, over 100. What am I doing here? All alone? In the middle of winter with the sun going down? What am I hoping to achieve? In some ways it was the perverse enjoyment of the challenge. My friend Zani doesn't really feel the cold. I feel it. I feel it in every fibre. It's not the cold I love; it's the swimming in it.

On very cold days I would abandon all formal training. I had cautiously returned to sets and warm-ups and cool-downs, and Mike – who runs the Durban Long Distance Swimming Association – would send me a weekly training programme comprising different sets and levels of exertion, in neat columns and different colours. I would print it out and put it into a plastic folder to prevent it getting wet. It got wet eventually anyway, and all the colours would merge into each other, but until then you could tell that blue was easy, pink was tough and green was suicide. When the sun dropped and the water was below 15 degrees, everything was at green level. Four hundred metres of pulling was impossible in that situation, my legs floating uselessly behind me; I may as well have thrown up a white flag to the Ice Goddess. Likewise, I would feel my lips and the tip of my nose go numb and watch my fingers turn yellow while holding a kickboard, my head and shoulders up in the air while my legs worked frantically behind me. Those were the days when the programme was consigned to the wet bag and I would swim as hard and as fast as I could to get warm. Even as the sun went down and the light faded, my arms and legs would work to a rhythm all their own. Mike understood.

What do you think about when you swim? Don't you get bored? Those are the questions I am asked most. The second is easier to answer than the first. Yes, I did get bored. I still do. The first hour is always the difficult one. It's cold, and it's difficult because it takes time to get going. My limbs flail awkwardly and I battle to find my rhythm. My mind plays along with my frustration. If you're battling now, it asks meanly, how are you going to swim for three or four or five hours? If you are cold 40 minutes into this swim, you won't be able to do the longer times and distances you say you want to do. Maybe you don't really want to do them. Maybe you just *think* you do. And maybe you are wrong. And even if you swim really fast, you won't be able to swim more than three kilometres per hour, and that means you will be in this pool for at least two hours and how cold will you be at the end of that? And if the sun was out, I would worry that I was cold even in the sunshine so, bizarrely, it was easier on the mind if the clouds owned the day. Right, I would think, there's no mercy out here today. Your back is against the wall. You'd better come out swinging. And I always did.

On days it was warm enough to follow the programme, the third set was – and is – the most difficult. The third set comes when I have swum enough to know which muscles are singing but still not enough to be halfway. That was always the lowest point of boredom, an exercise in mind control. In winter it was depressingly cold. In summer it was the set in which I had to get my heart rate up to an 80 per cent exertion level. Boring and hard. Terrible combination. Those minutes dragged like anything. I hate this, I would think; I am bored and my shoulders hurt and my neck aches and this is stupid and why am I even here, and if I was a real swimmer I would love this from the first length and I don't, and why didn't I do my rehab exercises before I started this session because now my neck is more sore and I'm probably making it worse and, and, and … But after the third set, or after 45 minutes, whichever came first, the boredom ebbed away and joy began. Joy crept up slowly and then burst into the pool and then there was just love and water and shine, even on the shortest days of winter. Then my mind would move into familiar grooves and my body would find its own rhythm and hold it. I once swam for five hours up and down a pool, never speeding up, never slowing down. Five hours, 12.3 kilometres. It was neither 12.5, nor 12.

I had a mental playlist and I ran through it over and over again, a bizarre selection of songs running through in my head. They have just one thing in common – they all match my stroke rate. I play them out in the same order. First Billy Joel's 'She's Always a Woman', into Carly Simon's 'Nobody Does It Better'. Then Phil Collins and Marilyn Martin with 'Separate Lives' from the *White Nights* soundtrack. There's some SafetySuit, a band very few people have heard of, and some Miley Cyrus, a singer very few people haven't heard of. There are about 10 songs on the list; they last 200 metres each and then I start again. Sometimes I break off and think about other things. Sometimes I don't think of anything at all except the sound of my breathing in the water and the way my shoulders feel. I have to remind myself to eat every hour or 45 minutes. Those are the rules. Whose rules? Mine.

But that was for a long daytime swim. Winter sunset swims were shorter and more brutal. At the end of every session would be a warm-down of 300 or 400 metres. That was difficult; I was already cold and slowing my heart rate down would make me colder. Also, it went against my every instinct to swim slowly in cold water. My natural response would be to get it over as quickly as possible.

One evening Sarah was standing at the edge of the pool watching me as I geared my mind up for those last few lengths. At least it was a 50-metre pool, and 400 metres equalled eight lengths. Eight lengths meant two songs. I could do it.

"Do those make you go faster?"

She pointed at my fins.

"Yep. You have to work a bit harder though."

I was biting my lips, trying to get some feeling into them so I could speak clearly.

She eyed me curiously.

"So why don't you do that last bit wearing them? Wouldn't it be easier?"

"Yep."

"So why don't you?"

I got ready to kick off.

"Because it would be easier."

Nothing worth it is easy.

185

The best part of a cold swim was the shower afterwards.

I once interviewed Jacob Dlamini about his book *Askari*, the story of an ANC operative who switched sides and began working for the apartheid government's security forces after he had been tortured for months. I asked the question, what would you do in that situation? Callers were enraged. Without exception, they called him a traitor. No matter what the torture, no matter what the extent of the pain, they would never switch sides; they would never inform on their colleagues and comrades and friends. Everyone was certain and, to a great degree, so was I. What kind of physical abuse could be worse than knowing you have turned on your friends? Wouldn't some kind of moral compass kick in at some point and push me to true north? Would that stop me from committing an act deemed unspeakable betrayal?

But lying on the floor of the shower, unable to turn on the hot tap, aching from the cold, shaking so badly I had bitten my tongue and blood was running out of my mouth and I couldn't stop it, I realised I couldn't be sure of that. In fact, I wondered what I wouldn't give up if someone was standing next to the taps with power over hot and cold? I knew I would beg for mercy. But I still went back, day after day. I still swam.

Once I got cold. Really, really cold. Sleepy and disoriented cold. I swam in winter rain and didn't realise how close I was to hypothermia until I tried to get out of the water and slipped back in. I waded to the steps and pulled myself out. I couldn't stand. Well done, Sam, I thought. *How much is enough? Just a little more.* I staggered to the showers, dropping my bag on the floor inside the door. I didn't think about it getting wet. I didn't think about anything at all except getting warm. In my desperation, I turned the hot and cold taps on full and lay down on the floor of the shower. I didn't know whether I was burning or freezing. I lay there for at least 15 minutes, waiting for feeling to return to my fingers, my toes, my heels, my face. It was horrible. Later, I sat in the car fully dressed dipping Provita into almond butter and eating them. I made a list of all the things I did that I wouldn't do again. Getting back into the pool wasn't one of them.

The drive home from the pool was one of the best parts of the day, the car heater turned up on high, warming up, the smell of chlorine mixed with moisturiser. The cold always seemed so far away and so manageable. The thought of wanting to get out of the water or of not wanting to get in in the first place felt like a distant dream. I'd usually spend the half-hour or 45 minutes in traffic stretching my neck and wondering what the next day's programme would feel like.

Swimming in the sea taught me surrender. So often in the confines of the swimming pool I would forget my own words: *always in charge, never in control.* When I was in the sea, all that changed. The sea did not care about me. It didn't love me or hate me. It was neither eager for me to succeed, nor did it plan for me to fail. The sea was just the sea. Seven months after the disaster that was Midmar, I went to Cape Town for the Cape Town Long Distance Swimming Association Awards evening and picked up my certificate and medal for the Robben Island swim in January. Back in my hotel room, I sat on the bed and studied them. I couldn't be proud. I felt like I should have been, but it was as though I had played a walk-on role in someone else's story.

The next day was Heritage Day and I decided to go down to Oceana Power Boat Club and swim in the Freedom Series swim that was taking place that morning. The Freedom Swim Series holds different events on certain public holidays and for this one you could choose between a one-mile or a three-point two-mile course. The day was grey, the wind nasty and sneaky and the sea rough. It was the first time I had been back to the sea to swim since Robben Island, and it was making no attempt to lure me back. I stood shivering in my costume and towel, watching registration and waiting for someone with a black pen to scribble a number on my arm.

Someone next to me said, "More than half the people here will only do one mile."

The course was on a loop.

There were a lot of people at the three-mile table so I didn't understand that.

"Most people will do the one and then get out because it's rough."

Oh, great.

As usual, I had picked great conditions for myself.

The water was 15 and the shock was horrible. I hadn't swum in anything under 27 in months. And those familiar feelings started all over again. What are you doing? Why are you here? And I wasn't excited at all – just worried and weary.

And then we swam.

I knew the waves were high because for most of the course I felt like I was swimming alone. Every now and again I would catch sight of a small group of colourful swimming hats and then the water would move again and I couldn't see them any more.

I had to breathe to one side because the waves kept smacking me in the face on the other and I got a mouthful of air to the left and a mouthful of water to the right. I also had to keep stopping to see where I was headed because I could see nothing in front of me. Whenever I thought I had found my groove, I was knocked back again. It was dark and cold and unpleasant, and suddenly I got very angry. I grew warm with rage. I had come back. I had tried again and for what? The water wasn't filled with love and dolphins. It was murky and unkind. And I was struggling and it didn't care. I rounded the first buoy, almost making contact with it, and fury drove me to the second. I hated everything about the swim. As I got to the second buoy, I stopped to tread water and get my bearings. The organiser, Derrick, had said the comeback marker was the Cape Town Stadium. The stadium is enormous. It's a 55 000-seater stadium. You can see it from everywhere. Except from where I was. I couldn't see it. I couldn't find my bearings at all. Where was everyone else? And then the swell moved and I saw it, directly in front of me. The waves were so high, I had to wait for it to come into view. It disappeared again and then reappeared. And in that moment all the anger ebbed away and I stopped fighting. The sea would always be stronger than me. I had no control over it. I could train as hard as I could, I could swim a hundred kilometres in a pool, but when I was in the ocean all of that mattered very little. All I could do was roll with it. And so I surrendered. Again. I had about 600 metres left and I enjoyed every stroke. I stopped struggling to bend it all to my will and went with the current. And eventually I was home.

The learning never stops. The second time I swam from Robben Island to Bloubergstrand the conditions were much the same as the first. The wind was low, the sun warm, the sea like glass. It was exactly the same. It was totally different. I had come such a long way in two years, I thought. I was strong, I was fit, and I was much faster. Eighteen months before, it had taken me two hours to swim five kilometres in the pool, now it took an hour and 49 minutes. Eleven minutes is a long time. Everything, from the weather to the wind speed to the water temperature, had come together to give me perfect conditions, and when you're going to swim a long way in very cold water that's what you need. Troy, another crazy cold-water swimmer, said to me once, "You have to make sure the odds are stacked in your favour because it's going to be hard anyway. But nothing worth it is easy." He's right.

When I woke up that morning I ticked off everything on my checklist. I packed my cap, my goggles, my spare goggles, two towels, food, water and warm clothes for afterwards. It may have been tracking 30 degrees that day but it took me a long time to warm up afterwards. Mike had the feeds ready to throw at me in a plastic bottle on a string every half an hour: a carbohydrate shake that styles itself as grape-flavoured but tastes nothing like grape and is designed to keep you going over long distances. It's not glamorous but it's very effective so I didn't have to worry about that. I ate a good, filling, wholesome breakfast of hot oats – and threw it up 10 minutes later.

I knelt on the bathroom floor in tears and wondered what on earth I had been thinking. How did I think I was going to do it again? It had all gone so wrong the first time. I remembered how scared I had been and how cold the water was and how I had battled, and two cold hands crept around my heart and an icy little voice breathed, "Let it go. You don't have to do this. You're not ready yet. You can stay here in the bathroom. You can tell everyone you're sick."

My phone screen flashed. Mike.

"Howzit, Sam! You ready?" He was so cheerful. I couldn't tell him the truth.

"Of course I am!"

My word, I sounded excited. Surely I must be – just a little?

"… past the bridge and I'll be waiting."

"Okay, I'll do that," I replied, not knowing what I'd just agreed to. I hadn't heard a word.

"You eaten breakfast yet?" he asked.

"I have," I said truthfully.

I left out the part about how I had almost immediately uneaten breakfast.

"See you just now," he said and rang off.

He was so confident.

And I made more oats and ate it. This time it stayed down.

When we got to the boat club, Mike left me to talk to Derrick, whose boat it was, and I stood and looked across the water at Robben Island.

It didn't seem very far away at all. It certainly didn't look 7.5 kilometres away. There was a haze over it, but you could make out its shape, the way it sat in the sea like a little flat mushroom top. And I felt a little curl of excitement in my stomach. It's Robben Island. It's going to be like swimming through blue velvet. There might be dolphins or whales! And Table Mountain would be on my right.

Toni Enderli was swimming that morning. He had swum the English Channel a few months previously, and today he was supporting a 17-year-old girl called Amy. She'd attempted a crossing a few months back in extremely rough conditions and hadn't managed to finish and now she was back to complete her attempt.

"Why did you try it if it was so rough?" I asked her later.

She shrugged.

"Well, partly because I really wanted to and partly because I

190

had told everyone I was going to and I didn't want to look as though I hadn't tried."

That was part of my problem the first time. Everyone knew. The swim had become public knowledge long beforehand. It's very hard to do the right thing for yourself when you're trying to please everyone else. This time was very different. This time almost no one knew.

Toni was stretching before the swim.

"This must seem easy to you after the Channel," I said to him.

He shook his head.

"This is never easy," he said.

I don't know what I wanted him to say. If he had said it was easy, would I have been more afraid?

"Could I swim with you to the island?" I begged.

In order for the swim to be recognised, you have to swim from the land. The rocks just off the island qualify as land, but you have to swim from the boat and swimming through the kelp to find one big enough to stand on can be tricky. Toni had done it often enough to be confident and I hoped some of his confidence would rub off on me.

Sometimes the words, "Man alive, I'd love a drink," pop into my head. When they do, it's seldom about the drink itself. It's about what it promises. A temporary relief from anxiety. A little pond of calm. After 14 years I know a promise isn't a commitment. But old thought patterns die hard.

"Sure you can swim with us," he grinned. He had no idea of the gift he'd just handed over.

On the way across to the island, the boat skimming the water, I held on to the straps on the side, trying not to brace every time we hit a wave. Lean into it, I said to myself. You can't fight it. You'll never win. It's the sea.

Over and over I reminded myself. Over and over. *It's not you. You can't own this.* As I've said over and over, the biggest lesson I learned the first time around was that the sea was just that. The sea. It didn't love me or hate me. It wasn't for me or against me. It just was. What happened in the sea was up to the sea. I could train and train. I could do fifties and hundreds until the battery went flat in my heart-rate monitor. I could practise in pools and dams and lakes, but in the end the success of any crossing would be determined not by me, but by the conditions on the day. I couldn't control wind, weather or temperature.

The sea was so blue and the sun was so bright and the sky around Table Mountain was cloudless. The water temperature off the island was just over 15 degrees. It was as though everything had come together in beautiful symmetry to give me the perfect day. But still that tiny voice was chipping at me.

"Imagine, after all this, you fail," it whispered. "You'll have absolutely no excuse. And everyone will know. You're not a swimmer. You're an imposter."

All the same demons were still there, perhaps even stronger because they had had two years to germinate and grow. And it had been a year of loss. My mother was dead. Could I still swim? Was I up to it?

It was the same shock when I eased into the water. Wow, this is real life. This is really happening. I could see the tips of the kelp moving on the surface of the water, thicker and thicker the closer you get to the island. Toni and Amy were already in the water. I can't remember who yelled, "Let's go!" but I think it was Toni. Actually, I'm sure it was Toni. Amy was very quiet and I was keeping my mouth firmly closed in case I was sick. I swam after them through the kelp, looking for a rock to stand on. Toni was having none of that.

"We start on the island!" he shouted happily.

Amy and I exchanged glances. I think we would have happily started on a rock nearby, but we followed him through the kelp. I don't like kelp. It feels slimy and rough at the same time, like someone with calloused hands trying to grab your legs.

We all came together on the shale at the edge of Robben Island. The old pier was on our left. I think we all held hands and Toni shouted, "Power!" It was the kind of moment that sounds very silly when you recount it but made beautiful crazy sense at the time.

And then we were in the water. I followed Toni and Amy back

through the kelp, and they went with their boat and I went with mine, trying not to think too hard about what might be living in that giant seaweed. But at least worrying about that kept me distracted. Once I was in open water it all came flooding back. All the worry and all the self-doubt, and a dam filled to bursting with despair. Suddenly it all seemed so far and so hard and so cold and so impossible. I couldn't even talk myself into it by telling myself how proud my mother would have been. I knew very well she wouldn't be proud at all. She would just be worried.

"But you've done this already, Sammy," she'd say. "Wasn't once enough?"

It's never enough.

So I started to swim for real – and I started hard. I needed to think, but I couldn't do that while I was treading water; I would just get cold. And I was cold already and the water felt as though it was getting colder.

"It's not getting colder, Sam," I kept telling myself. "It's in your head."

Yes, but my head was running the show and it was quite ready to throw in the towel by demanding a big fluffy one and a ride on a rubber duck to the beach and hot chocolate. I had to keep it in the water, just for the first hour. After that it would be all right. Just for an hour.

But an hour is a very long time.

One, two, three, breathe. Over one shoulder there was the other boat and Toni and Amy.

One, two, three, breathe. Over the other was my boat and Manly Mike. And Manly Mike was excited and enthusiastic enough for everyone. Even me. Especially me.

"If you can't do this first hour for you," I said to myself, "do it for him. Or at least 52 minutes."

Mike had support-crewed a big swim earlier in the year where the swimmer had lasted 51 minutes. I could manage 52.

He didn't know this. He just knew I was swimming in fantastic weather and there was a whale and there were dolphins. I didn't see the whale. Daniel, the pilot, told me there were dolphins.

"Don't worry, there are dolphins," he pointed out when I paused to swig my carbohydrate shake out of a plastic bottle on a piece of string. Real swimmers call this a feed.

I didn't know why he thought I would worry. Dolphins are lovely. I realised this when I saw them underneath me. For an occasional sea swimmer, one blue-grey fin looks much like another. And there were quite a few of them.

Some swimmers say that Table Mountain doesn't move as you swim. You keep looking to the right, but it stays put. I didn't have that. Table Mountain moved fast. I settled down after 40 minutes and paced the mountain. After an hour, I knew I was good. In my head, the swim officially moved from being Mike's thank-you to being mine again. Mike was still the most excited, though.

"You're doing well!" he yelled, hurling the bottle at me again. (I still suspect he aims it subconsciously.)

"I know," I said modestly. And then I looked back at the island.

That was nearly A Bad Moment. I had never looked back the first time. Not once. I was so cold and so afraid that I thought that if I looked back and the island was closer to me than I was to the beach, then I wouldn't be able to go on. I'd have stopped. This time I couldn't help myself. It seemed so far away and so close at the same time. I could see the lighthouse, but the shoreline was blurred. But, unlike Lot's wife, I didn't turn into a pillar of salt and dissolve. I kept swimming. It was all right. I was going to be all right.

"Time-wise, you're strong!"

That brought me back.

"How strong?" I was curious despite myself.

"Strong."

Okay, we would play it that way.

Then I was on my way. Two feeds meant I was over an hour in. The rest was a cruise. The playlist I hadn't been able to summon up suddenly unfroze itself and I remembered, in one big glorious bright flash, why I was here in the first place. It was to swim in the sea with Table Mountain on my right and Robben Island behind me and the skyline of Blouberg in front, and all the time the details of the buildings getting clearer and closer. Every now and again I paused to look around.

"Are you okay?" Mike would shout.

"Yes, I'm fine. I just want to see."

"But you've seen it all before!"

"Yes, but not like this."

I was like a seal, poking my head up and turning around to investigate at everything. I wasn't afraid; I was excited. I could see windows in the buildings and different colours and textures, and I could smell and taste the salt, and suddenly this long swim to freedom was nearly over. There's a gap in the rocks about 800 metres off shore and the temperature dipped to 14. But the rest was gravy. This time I wasn't tired or cold or sick. This time I could see the shapes of the buildings and the twin lights on the lifesavers' station, guiding me in. This time the strip of yellow, of gold, was a beach. This time when I stood up in the water it was by myself, although Mike was there and the boat pilots and other swimming friends past and present, all warm with love and encouragement. Seven and a half kilometres later I was more alive than when I had started. This time it was like a vitamin B shot. And everyone should have one of those once in a while.

This time my husband was happy.

"Well done, angel." Martin was warm and kind. But, yet again, my children were unimpressed.

"Did you go to where Nelson Mandela was in prison this time?" asked the 12-year-old.

"No, I didn't," I said hotly. "I only go to the edge of the island and I get in from there."

He raised blond eyebrows at me.

"So yet again you missed an opportunity."

"I'd look a bit silly wandering around the museum in a costume and goggles, wouldn't I?" I demanded. "And, anyway, I had seven kilometres to swim."

"You could have gone to the museum first and left your clothes on the boat afterwards if you really wanted to."

He has an answer for everything.

The nine-year-old was equally bored.

"Where did you come?"

"From Robben Island to the beach."

"No, where did you come *in the race*?"

"It wasn't a race. It was just me, swimming by myself."

A pause.

"Then why did you bother to do it?"

"Because I wanted to see if I could do it."

"But you did it once already."

"I wanted to see if I could do it again!"

And be conscious at the end of it.

She sighed.

"Did you get me a present?"

Straight to the important stuff. A life-changing event for me, a toiletry bag with penguins and an 'I heart Cape Town' logo on it for her.

Roger called me.

"Well done, my girl!" He was very excited. "It's because you put in the work!"

The work that I started with him, over two years before. The work that continued towards new goals for myself.

"Yes. Yes, I did," I said. "Are you going to swim tomorrow?"

Roger had a new apprentice. He had decided that every year he would help a swimmer fulfil their Robben Island dream – as long as they were prepared to train hard. He was still generous. Still intolerant of sloth.

"We are," he said happily. "The weather looks perfect."

And he did. And it was.

Just like mine.

CHAPTER 18

Forever

If I could go to the beach every day, I would. Whenever I am in Cape Town I go to the beach, no matter what the weather, even if it's to sit on a towel on the sand and watch the waves. Sometimes the waves are high and the sky is grey and the wind is cold, and sometimes the sun is high and the water laps gently around my ankles. The water's always cold. But I don't mind that. I expect it to be cold. The sea has been my greatest natural teacher. The sea throbs with life. It's not just water and waves and wind; there's a whole world under the surface. I get perspective from the sea.

I like to watch the waves. They remind me that life is a series of swells and some I can ride and some I must weather. But I am always in the sea. The sea makes me feel small. It is always and forever and I am only in the now. There are rules that I follow. I am careful and responsible. I don't swim in temperatures under 10 on a short swim and under 13 for a long one. Where others can do that easily with joy and without consequence, I cannot. I try to put on weight before a long swim in order to combat the cold. Other swimmers say it makes no difference whether you do or don't. It makes a difference to me. Those are boundaries I set for myself; I can't measure myself by someone else's methods or preferences. I don't expect anyone to approve of mine or follow me. We all have our own codes, our own ways of doing things. Some swimmers swear by fruit and potato to keep their energy levels up, others by jelly-babies and Milo. They are all right for themselves.

Swimming in the sea is like life. Life didn't change because I stopped drinking. The world went on exactly as it did before. I changed. I had to, or at least I had to change my behaviour, because if I hadn't, all those years ago, I don't think I would still be here. And I'm glad I am.

I realised early on in my sobriety that sobriety itself was going to have to be its own reward. Nobody loved me more for getting sober. Life didn't get easier to manage. In many ways, it was harder without a numbing agent. But nothing easy is worth it.

I get asked a lot about how I lost weight. People are disappointed when they hear it was a 10-year process, and in order for it to stay off it will be a process I will follow for the rest of my life. Those who find out I used to drink until I fell down ask me how I got like that. I don't have answers. Not even for myself. Only how not to do it any more.

A friend whose problem is cocaine still gets very angry about being an addict, despite having been clean for seven years.

"It's not fair, Sam," he rages. "It's not fair that other people can just do their shit and be fine and we can't."

"Life's not fair."

"Don't fucking say that! It doesn't help."

It doesn't help, no. He's right. Sometimes I want a drink. Once – and it was indeed just that *once* – I went camping with a group of friends and their children. I hated the idea and then when I got there I hated every minute. I hated the heat and the dust and the dirt and the insects and the communal bathrooms and the fact that the next people to arrive pitched their tents right next to ours. But most of all I hated the fact that within half an hour of us arriving the drinks were out.

"Seriously, the only way I am going to get through this is with wine. A lot of wine."

That was one of the more fastidious mothers. She thought we were glamping. We were not.

Another mother agreed.

A bottle was opened.

And then another one.

And then another.

And two hours later everyone else was fine.

I wasn't fine. I was mad as a snake. I was trapped in cattle-class hell while everyone else drank their way into First Class. Through beer and wine goggles, everything looks more positive. I know. I lived it.

"I think you're amazing, Sam," someone said. "I couldn't do this without a drink. I couldn't."

Couldn't you? Well, I have to. I actually have to. And not for the first or the last time, I was angry about that. I was angry that I couldn't have a drink, and even angrier that everyone else could and did. There are still phrases and sentences that touch a nerve with me.

"I just needed a drink ..." That's a big one.

No, my friend, you *wanted* a drink. I *need* one. And I cannot have one.

And even with a decade between then and the last drink, I still think it's fucking unfair. I still sometimes sit and wonder if I could have stopped it or changed its course. Sometimes I ask why, like a petulant child who cannot understand why she can't stay up late. Sometimes I wonder with a kind of academic distance. But it doesn't matter.

I tell my friend we're lucky. And I really think we are. Well, I am. Frustrating and difficult as it can be at times, I know what my demons are. All of them. Some people go their whole lives never knowing what triggers their more destructive behaviour. I do, and I would never have found out if I hadn't been forced to drink with those demons, gorge with them and then starve with them. It doesn't mean I have power over them; I have power only over my response to them. Hence the rules. Rules to drink by, rules to eat by, rules to swim by, rules to live by. Always rules.

I don't think being sober makes me a better person. I don't want or expect special treatment. I wasn't loved or shamed into sobriety. It is no one's fault that I got this way, or was born this way. And it is no one's responsibility but mine to take care of myself. I think alcoholism is a disease and I manage it, every day. Just for that day.

Alcoholism was my fault and it's my responsibility to manage it, and I know that. I've never expected any sympathy. I still don't. I still sometimes look for reasons for what triggered it, but I don't ever expect to find any. And they really don't matter now. Now it's about getting through one day at a time even though, as many alcoholics can attest to, a day can go by in a blink or it can be an eternity. I don't think of myself as special. I don't think addicts are special. I consider myself fortunate that some people can go their whole lives never working out what their demons are. I know mine. I live with it. It knows me. And we have to live together in uneasy harmony. It will never leave as long as I live; it is inside me and part of me, and I intend to live a long time.

We have our good days and bad days, but what we present and what we feel are often different. You can't tell when you put your feet in the water at Clifton how cold it's going to be just be looking at it. You have to feel it for yourself.

I have no answers to what to do next. I can tell you, in hindsight, how I know what I am, and I have, but I have no answers for others in similar positions or stages.

It's never over. The struggle continues. Although some days it isn't a struggle at all and some days it is difficult – from waking to sleeping, it's difficult. And I still take lots of medication, every day, to stay grounded and to keep the anxiety from taking hold of me and becoming debilitating, and I probably always will and I've had to make my peace with that. Someone asked me in a lift the other day if I attributed my success as a career woman to having a positive attitude. I told her that I thought it was that, combined with a carefully managed cocktail of antidepressants and anxiety-disorder medications, that made me the personification of female success she saw before her. I probably shouldn't have laughed afterwards. She got out on the next floor.

But every day is a new opportunity. Every day of sobriety is a gift. And so, whenever I can, I go back to the beach and sit on the sand and remember that even while life is sometimes very loud and very full, I can move myself through it. And I can move myself through it sober, one day at a time.

ee cummings said it best:

"for whatever we lose (like a you or a me), it's always ourselves that we find in the sea."

The story ends where it began, with my children. I told them about this book before I wrote it. I asked them if they minded if I told these stories.

"Will it be funny?" asked Chris.

"Parts of it will be," I promised.

"Will it be like a drama?" asked Genevieve.

"Oh, it will definitely be a drama," I assured her.

"Are we in it?" Ever the cautious one, my son.

"You are, but only in the good bits."

"Then do it, Mom." And Chris retreated into a Cressida Cowell book.

"Except, Mom, you have to do one thing. Promise." My nine-year-old was firm.

"What must I do?"

"You must write that I have long beautiful hair and green eyes."

And she does. So I have.